SUPERB
SIDE DISHES

Black Beans 'n' Rice, page 60

SUPERB
SIDE DISHES

© 2005 by Rodale Inc.

Printed in the United States of America
Rodale Inc. makes every effort to use acid-free ∞, recycled paper ♲.

Cover photographs: Mitch Mandel
Cover recipe: Fiesta Cornbread Courtesy of B&G Foods, page 116
Cover recipe: Fresh Beans & Tomatoes with Dill Cream Courtesy of Land O' Lakes, Inc., page 28
Cover recipe: Tomatoes Stuffed with Couscous Courtesy of Florida Tomato Committee, page 102
Food stylist: Diane Vezza
Illustrations: Judy Newhouse

Editorial Produced by:
BETH ALLEN ASSOCIATES, INC.

President/Owner: Beth Allen
Culinary Consultant/Food Editor: Deborah Mintcheff
Recipe Editor: Carol Prager
Project Editors: Stephanie Avidon, Melissa Moritz
Nutritionist: Michele C. Fisher, Ph.D., R.D.
Art Production Director: Laura Smyth (smythtype)
Photo Researcher: Valerie Vogel

Library of Congress Cataloging-in-Publication Data

Superb side dishes.
      p.   cm.
    Includes index.
    ISBN-13 978–1–59486–171–0 hardcover
    ISBN-10 1–59486–171–4 hardcover
    1. Side dishes (Cookery)   I. Rodale (Firm)
  TX740.S864   2005
  641.8'1—dc22   2004028426

2 4 6 8 10 9 7 5 3 1 hardcover

We inspire and enable people to improve their lives and the world around them

For more of our products visit **rodalestore.com** or call 800-848-4735

CONTENTS

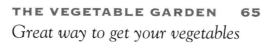

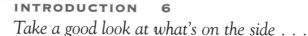

INTRODUCTION

Take a good look at what's on the side . . .

There's much more than salad and potatoes being served on the side these days . . . and for good reason. By definition, accompaniments like these are served on the side—to go along with, to enhance, or to make something better. That hasn't changed. But what has changed is how many different sides there are and where you'll find them: on the main dinner plate or in a little ramekin nestled on the dinner plate, on the salad plate, the bread and butter plate, or in no dish at all but simply on a buffet table as pick-me-up food. The size hasn't changed much, however; it's still on the small side—not as filling as the entrée, but always worth the effort when it's easy.

Another thing that hasn't changed—sides should always complement the rest of the meal in color, texture, and of course flavor. This means the potato or rice on the side with a delicate broiled sole filet should be mild and gently spiced, such as our Fruited Rice Pilaf (page 58), instead of hot, overpowering, and bold like a Cajun pilau. Here in *Superb Side Dishes* there are 100 great recipes as well as the mix-and-match philosophy that makes it simple, easy, and fast to round out each meal with the perfect go-along: that perfect side.

First, if you know the main dish you're serving tonight (such as the rest of the roasted chicken from last night's dinner), turn to the "What's for Dinner? Pick a Side" chart on page 15 and plan the rest of the meal at a glance. Make the Green Beans & Feta Salad (it's super-quick and ready in just 20 minutes!). Arrange it on dinner plates with the roasted chicken fanned out all around, and supper's on in less than half an hour. Choose the Garlic Mashed Potatoes (page 44) for Sunday's roast beef, plus a second side of Tender Popovers (page 110) "From the Bread Basket" to pass alongside. Another night, turn one of our "Substantial Sides" of Spinach Pie (page 100) into supper by serving it along with Mediterranean Tomato Salad on the side, of course (page 33).

Having hamburgers? Make a batch of Fun Fries (page 50) without standing over a skillet, then stir a pot of BBQ Baked Beans (page 62)—there's plenty to serve at least eight hungry folks. Another time, when you're having pork chops, simmer up some Scalloped Apples & Onions (page 131) to serve on the side.

The *Superb Side Dishes* book wouldn't be complete without some sweets that go along. No, these aren't desserts—they're that little something that is on the sweet side, yet falls somewhere between salad and dessert. When served with the main course, often right on the same plate, they round out the salty, savory, spicy, and tangy flavors of all the other foods. Apples, of course, are a natural—and dressed up with cranberries and walnuts, they're ready for the holidays (page 129). You'll find it also comes with its own *On the Menu* feature that helps you plan a memorable Thanksgiving feast. And a dish of Old-Fashioned Bread Pudding with Vanilla Sauce (page 134) makes any roast chicken dinner even more down-home and special. Plus, check out the *Time Savers* feature on page 132, from cooks just like you, for some great sauces to go with them.

Did you ever expect to be able to make a risotto fast? The Spring Risotto, under the special SuperQuick label, actually goes from grocery bag to dinner table in 30 minutes or less. And just as in all of The Quick Cook series, *Cooking Basics* brings you ready-references for "The Easiest Way to Seed a Tomato" (page 33) and "The Easiest Way to Roast Garlic" (page 44). One evening, why not pick up some baked ham and stir up a pot of Southern Collard Greens (page 76)?

To start discovering how *Superb Side Dishes* can bring excitement to your everyday meals, turn the page and read all about speedy "Sensational Sides." You'll find the basics—from what makes something a side to how to plan supper fast by using the "What's for Dinner?" chart on page 15. You'll also find out the impact that the "Blue Plate Special" had on serving balanced meals of "a meat and two sides" in America.

Just like the other Quick Cook books, we have teamed up with test kitchens and food professionals, plus cooking pros and food manufacturers all across the country, to bring you this collection of *Superb Side Dishes*, which, of course, contains over 100 reliable, tested recipes that come out perfect every time. And don't forget, there are lots of other books in The Quick Cook series, which will be coming your way soon. Each one is designed with its own special collection of just what you want in today's cookbooks—appetizing photographs, fast and fabulous recipes, and many never-fail tips and techniques.

So pick out one of the recipes, get out your favorite mixing bowl, and begin exploring the delicious foods that are off to the side these days—so much more delicious and varied than even a few years ago.

Cheddar-Stuffed Spuds, page 99

Sensational Sides

You get three sides with the roast chicken. I suggest the Southern corn pudding, stuffed tomatoes, and our sweet potato biscuits. And since it's Monday, Mattie baked her famous meat loaf—and it's perfect with some mashed potatoes, green beans, and her popping hot popovers." It's easy to see, side dishes can make the meal. They can be savory, spicy, or even sweet. Sides can arrive on the main dinner plate or on a dish off to the side. Some sides, like mac 'n' cheese, can turn into the main dish by doubling the serving or adding some chopped ham. But one thing all sides have in common: They must accompany and also complement the main entrée . . . and do it deliciously!

Herbed Bread Stuffing, page 90

Cheese Dipped Veggies, page 97

Savory Orzo, page 43

BLUE PLATE SPECIAL

Walk into almost any diner and look around: You're likely to see the daily Blue Plate Special posted on a blackboard. Tell your waiter, "Blue Plate, please," and you're in for a treat. In just a few minutes, a divided plate arrives brimming with the meat or fish of the day and two sides, likely a potato and a vegetable. It's guaranteed to be a goodly amount of delicious eating. But not only that, it comes at a special low price. In fact, it's very likely to be the most food for the least amount of money on the menu—and served the fastest. Just as likely, it's the chef's own special recipes—usually finger-lickin' down-home foods that are freshly cooked and make you very glad you stopped by for supper.

What comes on the Blue Plate varies with the state you're in and the day you're ordering. It could be roast pork and dressing in the Midwest, chicken 'n' dumplings in the Deep South, shrimp gumbo in New Orleans, or perhaps baked cod in New England. In most diners, the three most popular Blue Plates are always on the weekly menu, each served on the same day every week. Those three: roast turkey on top of stuffing, sliced roast beef and gravy, and homemade meat loaf—always served the Blue-Plate way, with a potato and a vegetable on the side.

The term *blue plate* dates back to at least the mid-1920s in America. As defined by Webster's, it is "a plate often decorated with a blue willow pattern, divided by ridges into sections for holding apart several kinds of food." Indeed, according to historians, some of the first Blue Plate Specials were actually served on a blue plate that was often decorated with the blue willow pattern. It was, and often still is, divided into three sections with ridges: a large one for meat and two identical smaller ones for a potato dish and a vegetable. In fact, over the years, the Blue Plate might well have been instrumental in teaching generations what a well-balanced meal looks—and tastes!—like, as well as the importance that sides make in rounding out a meal.

Order the Blue Plate Special today, and it's guaranteed you'll be paying more for it than in the 1920s. There's another change you can count on. The vegetables that came with those early specials were prepared the same way day after day: If it was potatoes, they were mashed; and if it was a green vegetable, it was peas, though sometimes carrots got mixed in. Today's Blue Plates still come with a meat or a piece of fish and two sides, though offerings are more varied. Instead of potatoes, you might get rice pilaf or honey-glazed yams; instead of peas, you might get stir-fried vegetables or creamed spinach. But one thing hasn't changed: The Blue Plate Special is guaranteed to be the best eats in the house!

WHAT MAKES A SIDE A SIDE?

What do a baked potato, a tomato salad, and a slice of spinach pie have in common? The answer's simple: Each is a side—that is, something to serve with an entrée to round out a delicious, balanced meal. And each, in its own way, matches up to the criteria of a perfect side (see page 13).

Cooking Basics

5 SIDES OF MAC 'N' CHEESE

Take the Traditional Macaroni & Cheese recipe on page 86. Vary the pasta or vary the cheese. Instead of 6 servings, plan on 4 main-dish servings. Supper's ready!

3-CHEESE PASTA BAKE:
Omit the Cheddar cheese and use 1 cup shredded Gruyere cheese (4 ounces), 4 ounces Brie cheese, and ¼ cup grated Parmesan cheese.

TEX-MEX MAC 'N' CHEESE:
For the cheese, use 1 cup shredded Cheddar cheese (4 ounces) and 1 cup Monterey Jack cheese with jalapeño peppers (4 ounces). Stir 1 pound cooked ground beef (85% lean) flavored with 2 teaspoons chili powder (or more to taste) into the macaroni and cheese mixture before baking.

CHICKEN & CHEESE: Omit the Cheddar cheese and use 2 cups shredded Jarlsberg cheese (8 ounces). Stir 2 cups chopped cooked chicken and ½ cup chopped scallions into the macaroni and cheese mixture and top with buttered fresh bread crumbs before baking, if you like.

CAJUN BAKE: Stir 1 pound cooked andouille sausage or hot pork sausage plus 1 cup sautéed green bell pepper into the macaroni and cheese mixture. Sprinkle the top of the casserole with paprika before baking.

SHRIMP 'N' MAC BAKE:
Omit the Cheddar cheese and use 2 cups shredded Havarti cheese (8 ounces). Stir in 2 cups coarsely chopped cooked shrimp (1 pound) plus ¼ cup chopped chives into the macaroni and cheese mixture before baking.

Irish Soda Bread, page 122

- Complements and layers flavor into the meal: Add a tangy vinaigrette or a sweet baked apple alongside slices of roasted pork.
- Brings color contrast to the meal: Some bright green asparagus and red cranberry chutney brighten up a piece of golden brown grilled chicken. Even white potatoes can add contrast to a plate of brown meat; for more contrast, shower them with green chives.
- Adds visual interest: A veal cutlet looks so much better (and more appetizing!) when served on a bed of farfalle (bow-tie pasta) tossed with a side of hot buttered green peas.
- Rounds out the meal: Adding a vegetable, a bread, a fruit, or a little something else that is sweet boosts nutritional value.

FEEDING THE SENSES

When picking that perfect side, keep the four senses in mind: smell, sight, taste, and touch. Here's how:

Consider flavors first. Naturally, the flavors of the side dish itself must be pleasing, balanced, and tasty—that is, something delicious you want to make and serve often. But that's not all. It has to complement, not compete with, the rest of the meal. Pair the various flavor components: sweet with sour, savory with salty, mild with spicy. For instance, serve mild-flavored baby greens with the bold flavor of lasagna.

Contrast textures. Pair crisp with creamy, such as foods with a crunchy topping with those that are gentle and soft. Toss up a side of Garden Fresh Coleslaw (page 21) to complement a main entrée of a grilled fish fillet.

Think color when choosing a side. Either contrast or complement the entrée. For example, to accompany slices of steak, think either green or red and serve a side of steamed asparagus or the Tomatoes Stuffed with Couscous from page 102.

Complement hot with cold. For instance, for a supper of cold sliced chicken, bake a batch of steaming hot Cheddar Onion Biscuits to serve on the side (page 107).

Increase appetite appeal before you take a bite! Use the serving of a side to make the meal look even more appetizing. Add a bed of baby greens to display a grilled chicken breast, then top with a second side of colorful grilled red bell peppers and zucchini.

Pair small and round with large and chunky. A side of tiny green peas teams up swell with plump rectangular dumplings and chunks of chicken.

Mexican Mini Quiches, page 92

Roasted Potatoes & Asparagus, page 34

Vegetable Fried Rice, page 59

THE SIZE OF A SIDE

As its name suggests, a side is bigger and more filling than a snack. Based on the guidelines established by the United States Department of Agriculture, the size of a side that is generally considered equal to 1 serving is:

- A side of salad = 1 cup tossed salad (including extras such as chopped tomatoes)
- A side of vegetables = ½ cup
- A side of fruits = ½ cup cut-up fruit or 1 medium fruit (such as a baked apple)
- A side of pasta, potatoes, or rice = ½ cup
- A side of beans = ½ cup
- A side of bread = 1 slice of bread or 1 biscuit, muffin, or roll
- A side of pudding = ½ cup (such as bread or rice pudding)
- A side of quiche = ⅛ of a 9-inch pie
- A side of a savory pie = ⅛ of a 9-inch pie

TURN A SIDE INTO SUPPER

Some side dishes are such favorites that home cooks have figured out how to add things to the recipe that turn the side into supper. Here are a few to try with your favorite recipes:

Ham 'n' Potatoes. Add bite-size pieces of baked ham to the Best Ever Potatoes au Gratin (page 48) before baking.
Hearty Pasta Toss. Turn that side of spaghetti into supper by doubling the pasta. Now double the pasta sauce and add 1 pound crumbled, cooked Italian sausage, stirring it into the sauce. Finish it off with fresh slivered basil on top of each serving.
Beyond Mac 'n' Cheese. Make the Traditional Macaroni & Cheese (page 86) with a hearty pasta, such as rotini (corkscrews) or radiatore ("little radiators"). Toss in some crisp crumbled bacon, smoked baked ham, or roasted chicken before baking.
Shrimp & Vegetable Stir-Fry. Prepare your favorite rice pilaf mix and stir in chopped cooked asparagus, sliced cooked carrots, and some cooked shrimp.

Cooking Basics

WHAT'S FOR DINNER? HERE'S A SIMPLE WAY TO PICK A SIDE

Planning dinner has never been quicker or easier! Just follow the chart and find great sides to serve along with whatever meat, poultry, or fish is on the menu tonight. Locate the entrée you're serving in the left column, then read across to find a side that matches up swell. Pick a side, turn to the recipe, and you're well on your way to dinner. Nothing could be faster or finer!

Entrée (main dish)	Side Salads	Pasta Potatoes & Rice	The Vegetable Garden	Substantial Sides	From the Bread Basket	Sweets on the Side
Beef (roasted or steak)	Broccoli Salad (page 31)	Easy Twice-Baked Potatoes (page 47)	Corn-on-the-Cob with Seasoned Butters (page 75)	Spinach Pie (page 100)	Tender Popovers (page 110)	Old-Fashioned Bread Pudding with Vanilla Sauce (page 134)
Chicken (roasted or grilled)	Roasted Potatoes & Asparagus (page 34)	Garlic Mashed Potatoes (page 44)	Speedy Creamed Spinach (page 81)	Corn Pudding (page 93)	Sweet Potato Biscuits (page 106)	Honey-Baked Apples (page 129)
Hamburgers	Garden Fresh Coleslaw (page 21)	Fun Fries (page 50)	Sweet & Hot Marinated Mushrooms (page 77)	Traditional Macaroni & Cheese (page 86)	Cheddar Onion Biscuits (page 107)	15-Minute Autumn Rice Pudding (page 136)
Meat Loaf	Green Beans & Feta Salad (page 30)	Cinnamon-Noodle Kugel (page 42)	Peas with Pizzazz (page 81)	Cheddar-Stuffed Spuds (page 99)	Asiago Bread (page 121)	Winter Fruit Compote (page 130)
Pasta	Salad Italiano (page 36)		Italian Vegetable Ragout (page 69)	Cheesy Stuffed Mushrooms (page 95)	Parmesan Garlic Bread (page 111)	Almond Tuile Cookie Cups (page 137)
Pork (roasted or chop)	Black Bean & Corn Salad (page 26)	Fruited Rice Pilaf (page 58)	Squash Bake (page 78)	Broiled Grits Wedges (page 88)	Cheese Twists (page 114)	Scalloped Apples & Onions (page 131)
Turkey (roasted)	Mixed Greens with Maple Dressing (page 20)	Candied Sweet Potatoes (page 54)	Brussels Sprouts with Lemon & Thyme (page 72)	Herbed Bread Stuffing (page 90)	Cranberry Almond Bread (page 120)	Caramelized Orange Flan (page 126)

Turkey 'n' Stuffin' Dinner. Prepare your favorite stuffing mix and stir in bite-size pieces of roasted turkey, shredded carrots, and cooked baby green peas.

Now start browsing through the pages of *Superb Side Dishes* and make a list of those you want to try. Here are a few of our favorites:

Black Bean & Corn Salad   (page 26)

Mediterranean Tomato Salad   (page 33)

Best Ever Potatoes au Gratin   (page 48)

Double-Baked Sweet Potatoes   (page 55)

Corn-on-the-Cob with Seasoned Butters   (page 75)

Cheddar Stuffed Spuds   (page 99)

Tender Popovers   (page 110)

Asiago Bread   (page 121)

Old-Fashioned Bread Pudding with Vanilla Sauce   (page 134)

Sweet Potato Pies   (page 138)

Tender Popovers, page 110

Corn-on-the Cob with Seasoned Butters, page 75

Sweet Potato Pies, page 138

Squash Bake, page 78

Fresh Beans & Tomatoes with Dill Cream, page 28

Side Salads

Here they are, all the easy salads you'd expect to find in a book like this—that ever-favorite coleslaw, a fresh tomato drizzled with vinaigrette, and one of those old-fashioned Italian tossed salads we all love. But this collection goes one step further. Many of these recipes do much more than just complement in the traditional sense: They make the meal. You'll find a black bean and fresh corn salad with a Tex-Mex twist that turns any barbecue into a fabulous feast. And a roasted potatoes and asparagus side salad that could stand in for the vegetable course in any meal. So get out your salad bowl and your whisk, and toss up one of these side salads for supper tonight.

MIXED GREENS WITH MAPLE DRESSING
Prep **15 MINUTES**

Maple Dressing (see recipe)

1 pound mixed salad greens (including spinach leaves)

¼ cup cubed cucumber

¼ cup shredded smoked Gouda cheese

Maple syrup adds just the right touch of sweetness to the salad dressing. For the best flavor, be sure to use pure maple syrup.

LET'S BEGIN Prepare the Maple Dressing.

TOSS & SERVE Put the salad greens in a large serving bowl and drizzle with the dressing. Add the cucumber and cheese and toss to mix well.

MAPLE DRESSING
Whisk ¼ cup maple syrup, 2 tablespoons lemon juice, and 2 table-spoons canola oil together in a small bowl. Add salt and ground black pepper to taste.

Makes 8 servings

Per serving: 81 calories, 2g protein, 9g carbohydrates, 4g fat, 1g saturated fat, 4mg cholesterol, 76mg sodium

GARDEN FRESH COLESLAW

Prep **25 MINUTES**

To add even more good taste to this coleslaw, stir ¼ to ½ teaspoon celery seeds, dried dill weed, or dried tarragon, crumbled, into the dressing.

Zesty Coleslaw Dressing (see recipe)

3   **oranges, peeled, cut into bite-size pieces, and well drained**

1   **small head cabbage, thinly sliced**

1   **carrot, shredded**

1   **small green bell pepper, shredded**

¼   **cup thinly sliced scallions**

1   **orange, sliced (optional)**

Green bell pepper rings (optional)

LET'S BEGIN Prepare the Zesty Coleslaw Dressing. Combine the remaining ingredients in a large bowl. If not serving immediately, cover and refrigerate the dressing and the salad until chilled.

TOSS AND SERVE Right before serving, add the dressing to the salad and toss to mix well. Garnish with the orange slices and bell pepper rings, if you like.

ZESTY COLESLAW DRESSING

In a small bowl combine ½ cup mayonnaise or salad dressing, the grated zest of 1 orange, 2 tablespoons orange juice, 1 tablespoon sugar, ¼ teaspoon salt, and ¼ teaspoon ground white pepper. Stir until well blended.

Makes 8 servings
Per serving: 115 calories, 2g protein, 18g carbohydrates, 5g fat, 1g saturated fat, 4mg cholesterol, 200mg sodium

Cook to Cook

WHAT ARE SOME DIFFERENT WAYS TO MAKE COLESLAW?

"My classic coleslaw consists of **lots of finely shredded green cabbage,** some chopped parsley, a shredded carrot or two, and a creamy mayonnaise-based dressing that is zipped up with a bit of vinegar, salt, and pepper.

I also sometimes shred Napa cabbage and mix it with thinly sliced red and yellow bell peppers, then **dress it with store-bought or homemade peanut sauce.**

For a change of pace I like to make fennel slaw. I very thinly **slice fresh fennel using my vegetable slicer** and toss it with matchstick strips of green apple and a mustardy salad dressing.

When I want a slaw that is light and refreshing, I make my basic mix of cabbage and carrot and **toss it with a dressing that's made from half mayonnaise and half sour cream.** Then I spiff it up with poppy seeds and a generous amount of freshly grated lemon zest. It's my favorite side dish for grilled salmon. "

SOUTH OF THE BORDER SLAW
Prep **15 MINUTES**

1   package (16 ounces) coleslaw mix

½   pound fresh peeled pineapple, cut into thin wedges

½   cup reduced-fat Italian salad dressing

3   to 4 tablespoons chopped fresh cilantro

1   garlic clove, crushed through a press

1   teaspoon ground cumin

¼   teaspoon salt

Corn chips (optional)

Everyone's favorite—coleslaw—gets even better when the refreshing flavors of the Southwest come into play. When buying fresh cilantro, look for leaves that are bright green and not wilted or yellowing.

LET'S BEGIN Combine the coleslaw and pineapple in a large bowl.

MIX IT UP Stir the dressing, cilantro, garlic, cumin, and salt together in a small bowl.

TOSS & SERVE Pour the dressing mixture over the salad and toss to mix well. Sprinkle the corn chips on top, if you like.

Makes 6 servings

Per serving: 47 calories, 1g protein, 11g carbohydrates, 0g fat, 0g saturated fat, 0mg cholesterol, 379mg sodium

SuperQuick

SHRIMP & BEAN SALAD

Prep **20 MINUTES**   *Cook* **3 MINUTES**

1	pound large shrimp, peeled and deveined
½	cup roasted garlic vinaigrette salad dressing
¼	teaspoon salt
⅛	teaspoon red-pepper flakes
½	cup thinly sliced red onion
1	can (15 ounces) cannellini or small white beans, rinsed and drained
⅛	teaspoon ground black pepper
8	large romaine lettuce leaves

This super tasty salad is also great when served all tossed together. It's an easy recipe to double or even triple to serve to a hungry crowd.

LET'S BEGIN Combine the shrimp with 2 tablespoons of the dressing, the salt, and pepper flakes in a bowl. Heat a large skillet over high heat. Add the shrimp mixture and cook, stirring occasionally, for 2 minutes, or until the shrimp are light golden. Stir in the onion and ¼ cup of the dressing.

TOSS & SERVE Combine the beans with the black pepper and the remaining 2 tablespoons dressing in a medium bowl and toss to mix well. Arrange the lettuce on a platter, then top with the shrimp and bean mixtures.

Makes 4 servings
Per serving: 355 calories, 32g protein, 32g carbohydrates, 11g fat, 11g saturated fat, 172mg cholesterol, 814mg sodium

---

Time Savers

FAST-COOKING THE BEANS

Using canned beans is a real time saver, but it is hard to beat the texture and flavor of freshly cooked dry beans. Plus they're especially easy on the wallet.

If you plan ahead, beans can be soaked overnight, but if you haven't done that, here's our method for quick-soaking beans.

• Put the desired amount of beans in a saucepan and cover with 2 inches of cold water.

• Bring the pot to a boil and let the beans cook for 3 minutes.

• Remove the pan from the heat, cover it, and let it stand for 1 hour. Drain and rinse the beans. They're ready to cook in any recipe that calls for beans that have been soaked overnight.

PINEAPPLE BLACK BEAN SALAD

Prep **15 MINUTES**

2	cups fresh pineapple chunks
1	can (14 to 16 ounces) black beans, drained and rinsed
1½	cups cooked brown rice
1½	cups cubed cooked chicken breast
1	medium red, yellow, or green bell pepper, chopped
½	cup chopped celery
½	cup chopped scallions
½	cup fat-free or light honey Dijon salad dressing

Here's a simple and creative way to serve this bold-colored and flavored side salad: Spoon it into dried corn husks, which are readily available in specialty food stores, and garnish with chile peppers.

LET'S BEGIN Stir all of the ingredients except the dressing together in a large bowl.

TOSS IT UP Add the dressing to the salad and toss to mix well.

Makes 8 servings

Per serving: 206 calories, 18g protein, 42g carbohydrates, 2g fat, 1g saturated fat, 32mg cholesterol, 204mg sodium

SuperQuick
Black Bean & Corn Salad

Prep **15 MINUTES**

2	cans (19 ounces each) black beans, rinsed and drained
3	cups cooked fresh whole-kernel corn or canned whole-kernel corn
1	small green bell pepper, diced
⅓	cup chopped fresh cilantro
¼	cup canola oil
2	tablespoons red wine vinegar
1	garlic clove, minced
½	teaspoon ground cumin
½	teaspoon sugar

Salt and ground black pepper

8	cherry tomatoes, halved

This is a fabulous salad to serve alongside grilled chicken or fish or even your favorite barbecued ribs. It can be made at least 4 hours ahead and refrigerated until you are ready to serve it.

LET'S BEGIN Stir the first 4 ingredients together in a large bowl.

MIX & BLEND Whisk the oil, vinegar, garlic, cumin, and sugar in a small bowl. Season to taste with salt and pepper.

TOSS & SERVE Pour the dressing over the bean mixture and toss to mix well. Stir in the tomatoes just before serving.

Makes 8 servings
Per serving: 230 calories, 9g protein, 34g carbohydrates, 7g fat, 1g saturated fat, 0mg cholesterol, 460mg sodium

EASY THREE-BEAN SALAD

Prep **10 MINUTES + CHILLING**

Grated zest of ½ lemon

¼   cup lemon juice

1   envelope (0.6 ounce) Italian salad dressing mix

2   tablespoons water

⅔   cup vegetable oil

1   can (16 ounces) cut green beans, drained

1   can (15 ounces each) red kidney beans and chickpeas, drained and rinsed

1   small onion, sliced and separated into rings

Salad greens

To get ¼ cup of lemon juice, you will need about 2 large lemons. Look for lemons that are smooth-skinned and heavy for their size for the most juice. And be sure to wash and dry the lemons well before grating them.

LET'S BEGIN Combine the lemon zest and juice, dressing mix, and water in a jar. Cover tightly and shake well. Add the oil and shake well again until blended.

TOSS IT UP Combine the beans, chickpeas, and onion in a large bowl. Add the dressing and toss to mix well. Cover and refrigerate until chilled. Serve on salad greens.

Makes 6 servings

Per serving: 397 calories, 9g protein, 36g carbohydrates, 26g fat, 3g saturated fat, 0mg cholesterol, 1,113mg sodium

---

Cooking Basics

8 FAVORITE AND FLAVORFUL BEANS

Do you know your beans?

BLACK BEANS, or turtle beans, are the base of black bean soup and are also used in burritos.

CRANBERRY BEANS, also known as shell beans, are cream colored and have red streaks that disappear during cooking. These beans have a lovely nutty flavor.

GREAT NORTHERN BEANS are small white beans with a subtle flavor.

LIMA BEANS are also called butter beans. They are rather large and greenish beige and hold their shape well when cooked.

NAVY BEANS are small white beans that are also known as Yankee beans. They are used in pork and beans, Boston baked beans, and soups.

PINTO BEANS are named for the Spanish word "speckled," which is what they are.

RED KIDNEY BEANS are a popular all-purpose bean that has dark red skin. Their flesh is pale, and they have an almost sweet flavor and slightly mealy texture.

WHITE KIDNEY (CANNELLINI) BEANS are a milder version of red kidney beans. They're often used in Italian cooking in salads, soups, and in pastas.

FRESH BEANS & TOMATOES WITH DILL CREAM

Prep **20 MINUTES + CHILLING**

1   cup reduced-sodium
     chicken broth

½   pound green beans,
     trimmed (2 cups)

½   pound yellow wax beans,
     trimmed (2 cups)

Dill Cream (see recipe)

3   plum tomatoes, sliced

The beans can be cooked and refrigerated up to a day ahead, if you like. And the dressing can be stirred together and refrigerated as well. Just be sure to slice the tomatoes just before serving.

LET'S BEGIN Pour the broth into a large skillet and bring to a full boil over medium-high heat. Reduce heat to medium and add the beans. Cover and cook for 10 to 15 minutes, until the beans are crisp-tender. Drain. Cover and refrigerate at least 30 minutes, or until chilled.

MAKE IT SAUCY Meanwhile, prepare the Dill Cream and refrigerate.

SERVE Arrange the beans and tomatoes on a large platter. Spoon the Dill Cream over the vegetables.

DILL CREAM

In a small bowl combine ¼ cup sour cream, 2 chopped scallions, 1 tablespoon milk, 1 teaspoon Dijon mustard, ¼ teaspoon dried dill weed, ⅛ teaspoon ground black pepper, and a dash of salt. Stir to mix well. Cover and refrigerate if not using immediately.

Makes 6 servings
Per serving: 100 calories, 7g protein, 10g carbohydrates, 5g fat, 2g saturated fat, 5mg cholesterol, 55mg sodium

GREEN BEANS & FETA SALAD

Prep **10 MINUTES**   *Cook* **10 MINUTES**

8	ounces green beans, trimmed
⅓	cup olive oil vinaigrette salad dressing
2	tablespoons chopped fresh cilantro or mint (optional)
1	tablespoon chopped shallot or onion
¼	teaspoon salt
⅛	teaspoon ground black pepper
⅛	teaspoon grated lemon zest
1	large head Boston lettuce, torn into bite-size pieces
1	package (4 ounces) crumbled feta cheese

Serve this easy and refreshing salad as a side dish to any simply grilled meat, fish, or poultry, or enjoy it as a light lunch on a warm summer's day. The easiest way to trim green beans is to simply snap off the stem ends.

LET'S BEGIN Bring a medium saucepan of water to a boil. Add the green beans and cook for 6 minutes, or until crisp-tender. Drain and rinse with cold water until completely cool.

TOSS IT UP Put the green beans, 2 tablespoons of the dressing, the cilantro, if you like, the shallot, salt, pepper, and lemon zest in a medium bowl and toss to mix well.

SERVE Right before serving, add the remaining dressing to the lettuce in a large bowl and toss to mix well. Arrange the lettuce on a platter. Top with the green bean mixture and sprinkle with the cheese.

Makes 4 servings

Per serving: 196 calories, 6g protein, 8g carbohydrates, 16g fat, 6g saturated fat, 17mg cholesterol, 466mg sodium

BROCCOLI SALAD

Prep **10 MINUTES + CHILLING**

6	cups broccoli florets
1	cup thinly sliced celery
½	cup raisins
¼	cup sunflower seeds
½	cup mayonnaise
⅓	cup sugar or honey
¼	cup plain nonfat yogurt
2	tablespoons distilled white or cider vinegar

Serving broccoli in a salad is such a refreshing and unusual way to enjoy this healthful and tasty vegetable. To save time, buy precut florets.

LET'S BEGIN Combine the broccoli, celery, raisins, and sunflower seeds in a large bowl.

TOSS & CHILL To make the dressing, whisk the remaining ingredients together in a small bowl until smooth. Add to the broccoli mixture and toss well. Cover and refrigerate for at least 2 hours to allow the flavors to mellow.

Makes 6 servings

Per serving: 227 calories, 5g protein, 33g carbohydrates, 10g fat, 1g saturated fat, 5mg cholesterol, 194mg sodium

SUNNY CARROT SALAD

Prep **15 MINUTES + CHILLING**

1	package (16 ounces) frozen sliced carrots
1	can (20 ounces) pineapple tidbits or crushed pineapple, drained, juice reserved
1	tablespoon cornstarch
3	scallions, thinly sliced
2	tablespoons fresh parsley, minced
2	tablespoons minced crystallized ginger
¼	teaspoon salt

Pinch of ground black pepper

With just 15 minutes of prep time, this dish is ideal for a buffet table to serve alongside roast turkey or baked ham.

LET'S BEGIN Cook the carrots according to package directions. Combine with the pineapple in a large bowl.

COOK IT QUICK Whisk the reserved pineapple juice and cornstarch together in a small saucepan until blended. Bring to a boil over medium-high heat, stirring constantly. Cook for 1 minute, or until the sauce thickens and boils. Remove from the heat and stir in the scallions, parsley, ginger, salt, and pepper.

TOSS & CHILL Add the juice mixture to the carrots and pineapple and toss to mix well. Cover and refrigerate for 4 to 6 hours, until chilled.

Makes 8 servings

Per serving: 75 calories, 1g protein, 19g carbohydrates, 0g fat, 0g saturated fat, 0mg cholesterol, 114mg sodium

Orange & Beet Salad

Prep **30 MINUTES + CHILLING**

2   cans (14½ ounces each) sliced beets, drained

2   teaspoons grated orange zest

2   oranges, peeled and cut into sections

½   red onion, cut into ⅛-inch-thick wedges

¼   cup Dijon mustard

3   tablespoons red wine vinegar

1   tablespoon olive oil

1   tablespoon honey

¼   teaspoon salt

¼   teaspoon ground black pepper

Beet and orange is a classic combination that can't be beat for great flavor and great color. For ease, be sure to grate the orange zest before peeling the oranges.

LET'S BEGIN Combine the beets, orange zest, orange sections, and onion in a large bowl.

MIX IT UP Whisk all of the remaining ingredients together in a small bowl.

TOSS & CHILL Drizzle the dressing over the salad and toss to coat. Cover and refrigerate for 30 minutes.

Makes 6 servings

Per serving: 110 calories, 4g protein, 21g carbohydrates, 3g fat, 0g saturated fat, 0mg cholesterol, 603mg sodium

MEDITERRANEAN TOMATO SALAD

Prep **10 MINUTES + CHILLING**

3	pounds assorted tomatoes (plum, yellow, or beefsteak), cut into wedges, or cherry tomatoes, halved
½	cup balsamic or olive oil vinaigrette salad dressing
¼	cup loosely packed fresh basil leaves, cut into thin strips
1	large shallot or small onion, finely chopped
	Salt and ground black pepper (optional)
	Parmesan cheese shavings (optional)

Make a dramatic-looking salad by topping it with Parmesan shavings. Create them by drawing a vegetable peeler along the length of the Parmesan wedge. To keep them fresh tasting, make the shavings just before serving the salad.

LET'S BEGIN Combine the tomatoes, dressing, basil, and shallot in a large bowl and toss to mix. Cover and refrigerate for at least 30 minutes, or until chilled.

SERVE Right before serving, season with salt and pepper and sprinkle with the cheese shavings, if you like.

Makes 6 servings

Per serving: 105 calories, 2g protein, 12g carbohydrates, 6g fat, 1g saturated fat, 0mg cholesterol, 245mg sodium

---

Cooking Basics

THE EASIEST WAY TO SEED A TOMATO

Sometimes a recipe calls for removing the seeds and the juice from a tomato. This is often done to prevent the juice from making a food, such as a pizza, soggy. Seeding a tomato is really simple and easy once you know how.

Cut the tomato crosswise in half. Hold one half in your hand

and gently squeeze the tomato while holding it over a bowl (if you're saving the juice) or over the sink (if you're not). Now take a peek. If some of the seeds haven't fallen out, shake the tomato a couple of times or use your fingers to finish the job. You're done . . . that's all there is to it!

ROASTED POTATOES & ASPARAGUS

Prep **20 MINUTES**   *Bake* **30 MINUTES**

½   cup Italian salad dressing

⅓   cup Dijon mustard

2   pounds small red potatoes, scrubbed and halved

2   cups cut-up fresh or frozen asparagus

2   cups grape or cherry tomatoes, halved

⅓   cup sliced scallions

If you want to make this dish ahead, prepare it up to the point where the tomatoes and scallions get tossed in. Gently reheat the dish in the microwave on Medium just until heated through, then stir in the tomatoes and scallions.

LET'S BEGIN Preheat the oven to 350°F. Spray a jelly-roll pan with cooking spray.

INTO THE OVEN Whisk the dressing and mustard together in a large bowl. Combine ¼ cup of the dressing mixture and the potatoes in a medium bowl. Arrange the potatoes on the baking pan. Bake for 20 minutes. Remove the pan from the oven and add the asparagus. Bake 10 to 15 minutes longer, until the potatoes are tender when pierced with a fork and the asparagus is light brown.

TOSS & SERVE Transfer the potatoes and asparagus to the remaining dressing mixture in the bowl. Stir in the tomatoes and scallions. Serve warm or at room temperature.

Makes 6 servings
Per serving: 200 calories, 7g protein, 33g carbohydrates, 6g fat, 1g saturated fat, 0mg cholesterol, 655mg sodium

SPINACH & ASPARAGUS SALAD

Prep **25 MINUTES**

The fruitfully delicious dressing is one you will find lots of uses for, including drizzling over sliced cooked chicken and spooning over a simple mixed green salad.

Strawberry Dressing (see recipe)

8   **cups loosely packed trimmed fresh spinach**

1   **pound asparagus, blanched and drained**

4   **tablespoons toasted slivered almonds**

LET'S BEGIN Prepare the Strawberry Dressing, cover, and refrigerate.

DRIZZLE & SERVE Arrange the spinach on 4 plates. Top each with one-fourth of the asparagus and drizzle with about ⅓ cup of the dressing. Sprinkle each with 1 tablespoon almonds.

STRAWBERRY DRESSING

Put in the bowl of a food processor or blender: 1 cup hulled strawberries, ½ cup orange juice, 2 tablespoons raspberry vinegar, 2 tablespoons extra-virgin olive oil, 4 teaspoons honey, and ¼ teaspoon salt. Process, pulsing on and off, until slightly chunky. Cover and refrigerate.

Makes 4 servings

Per serving: 195 calories, 7g protein, 20g carbohydrates, 12g fat, 1g saturated fat, 0mg cholesterol, 327mg sodium

---

Cook to Cook

WHAT'S THE BEST WAY TO GET SPINACH CLEAN?

❝I love the flavor of fresh spinach, but *it takes an extra bit of effort to remove all of the dirt and grit,* especially if the spinach is the curly variety. Here's how I do it with ease:

Fill the sink with *cool—not cold—water.* Plunge in the spinach and swish it around several times to help shake the grit loose.

Lift out the spinach and *place it in a colander,* then drain out the water along with the grit.

Fill the sink again with water and rewash the spinach. You know you have done a good job when no grit accumulates in the bottom of the sink.

And don't forget, even if you buy bagged spinach that is labeled prewashed, it is still a good idea to wash it at home.❞

SuperQuick
SALAD ITALIANO

Prep **10 MINUTES**

1   package (10 to 11 ounces) hearts of romaine (about 8 cups torn lettuce leaves)

1   package (8 ounces) white mushrooms, sliced

4   slices provolone cheese (4 ounces), cut into strips

1   medium tomato, cut into wedges

½   cup thinly sliced red onion

½   cup Caesar or creamy roasted garlic salad dressing

Serve this zesty salad alongside a plate of sliced salami, ham, and turkey for a simple and delicious feast!

LET'S BEGIN Combine the romaine, mushrooms, cheese, tomato, and onion in a large bowl. If not serving immediately, cover and refrigerate up to 2 hours.

TOSS & SERVE Right before serving, add the dressing and toss to mix well.

Makes 6 servings

Per serving: 200 calories, 7g protein, 5g carbohydrates, 17g fat, 5g saturated fat, 13mg cholesterol, 385mg sodium

TABBOULEH SALAD

Prep **20 MINUTES**   *Cook* **2 HOURS**

This refreshing grain and vegetable salad is a staple in the Middle East. Go native and toss in a generous handful of chopped fresh mint and serve the salad with toasted pita bread triangles.

3	cups water or vegetable or chicken broth
¼	teaspoon salt
1	cup hulled (whole grain) barley
3	chopped scallions
2	chopped tomatoes
1	chopped cucumber
¼	cup chopped fresh parsley
¼	cup canola oil
¼	cup lemon juice

LET'S BEGIN Bring the water and salt to a boil in a medium saucepan. Stir in the barley. Reduce the heat to low. Cover and simmer for 2 hours, or until the liquid has been absorbed and the barley is tender.

TOSS & SERVE Transfer the barley to a large bowl and cool. Stir in the scallions, tomatoes, cucumber, and parsley. Add the oil and lemon juice and toss well.

Makes 8 servings

Per serving: 160 calories, 4g protein, 21g carbohydrates, 7g fat, 1g saturated fat, 0mg cholesterol, 82mg sodium

Food Facts

THE TALE OF TABBOULEH

Tabbouleh is a grain salad commonly enjoyed throughout Middle Eastern countries. It's full of flavor and very colorful. Tabbouleh is made with bulgur wheat—a nutritious staple containing wheat kernels that have been steamed, dried, and crushed. Bulgur is chewy but tender at the same time and is available in coarse, medium, and fine grains.

Tabbouleh is the popular salad made from cooked bulgur that is tossed with chopped tomato, chopped cucumber, lots of fresh mint and parsley, plus a refreshing amount of lemon juice. After making this salad, you can keep it in a covered container in the refrigerator for 2 days.

Spring Risotto, page 57

Pasta, Potatoes & Rice

Time was, not so long ago, a balanced meal meant a meat, a potato, and a vegetable. But things have changed. We now know that same meal can be just as balanced, nutritionally speaking, if on some days the potato is replaced with fried rice, polenta, or even a hearty helping of barbecued baked beans. Here's your chance to try a Sweet Potato Soufflé, a Cinnamon-Noodle Kugel, or the fastest and easiest risotto ever! But don't worry, the ever-loved potato is not forgotten. Slice it into a gratin to take to your neighbor's cookout, make it into fries without much fuss or muss, or bake it twice and stuff it back into its shell to go along with the Sunday roast. These sides will get raves—guaranteed!

POLENTA WITH TOMATO SALSA

Prep **45 MINUTES + STANDING**   *Cook* **35 MINUTES**

Tomato Salsa (see recipe)

7 cups chicken stock or broth

2 cups coarse-grained yellow cornmeal

¼ cup finely chopped fresh basil

2 tablespoons grated Parmesan cheese

1 tablespoon butter

¼ pound wild greens or mixed salad greens

The basic polenta can be cooked up to 4 hours ahead, which is most of the prep. Grill and serve with salsa—delicious!

LET'S BEGIN Butter a jelly-roll pan and set aside. Make the Tomato Basil Salsa and set aside. Bring the stock to a boil over high heat. Slowly add cornmeal in a steady stream, stirring constantly. Cook, stirring constantly with a wooden spoon, until the mixture returns to a boil.

SIMMER & STIR Reduce heat to medium and let simmer, stirring, for 20 to 30 minutes, until the cornmeal pulls away from the sides of the pan in a mass. Stir in the basil, cheese, and butter until the butter melts. Pour the polenta into the jelly-roll pan. Set aside to cool. Cut into twelve 3-inch squares, then cut each square into 2 triangles.

GRILL & SERVE Preheat the grill or heat a large nonstick skillet. Grill the polenta until golden, turning once. Serve immediately on top of the greens, and spoon some Tomato Basil Salsa on top.

TOMATO SALSA

In a large bowl combine: 2 large chopped ripe firm red tomatoes, 1 chopped large red onion, one 10-ounce package frozen corn (thawed), 2 cups cooked black beans (or one 15-ounce can, drained), 1 chopped medium red bell pepper, ¼ cup olive oil, 1 tablespoon balsamic vinegar, 4 cloves minced garlic, 1 small diced jalapeño pepper (cored and seeded), a dash of red-pepper flakes, ½ teaspoon salt, ¼ teaspoon freshly ground black pepper, and a dash of hot pepper sauce. Stir until mixed. Set aside at room temperature while preparing polenta. Stir in 1 cup slivered fresh basil right before serving.

Makes 6 servings (4 triangles each)

Per serving: 440 calories, 15g protein, 68g carbohydrates, 14g fat, 3g saturated fat, 10mg cholesterol, 1,436mg sodium

PINEAPPLE WILD RICE

Prep **15 MINUTES**   *Cook* **1 HOUR**

- 1 cup brown rice
- ½ cup wild rice
- ¼ cup margarine
- 2 cups sliced white mushrooms
- 1 large onion, chopped (1 cup)
- 1 teaspoon chopped fresh thyme or ¼ teaspoon dried, crumbled
- 1 cup finely chopped fresh pineapple
- 1 cup finely chopped dried apricots
- ½ cup toasted pine nuts

Fresh thyme sprigs (optional)

Serve this flavorful side with roasted leg of lamb or with broiled lamb chops and steamed green beans. Then end the meal with store-bought fruit pie or tart and a bowl of softly whipped cream.

LET'S BEGIN Cook the brown and wild rice according to package directions, omitting any fat.

INTO THE PAN Melt the margarine in a large skillet over medium-high heat. Add the mushrooms and onion and cook for 10 minutes, or until the onions are tender.

STIR & SERVE Stir in the thyme, pineapple, apricots, and pine nuts until blended. Stir in the brown and wild rice. Cook, stirring, until heated through. Serve hot or at room temperature. Garnish with thyme sprigs, if you like.

Makes 10 servings

Per serving: 219 calories, 6g protein, 31g carbohydrates, 9g fat, 2g saturated fat, 0mg cholesterol, 57mg sodium

CINNAMON-NOODLE KUGEL

Prep **15 MINUTES**   *Bake* **35 MINUTES**

8	ounces egg noodles, cooked according to package directions
4	ounces Neufchâtel cheese
½	cup nonfat ricotta cheese
½	cup sugar
4	large eggs
1	cup nonfat or low-fat milk
½	cup butter or margarine, melted
½	teaspoon ground cinnamon + extra for topping (optional)

Noodle kugel (pudding) tastes delicious any time of day. In fact, it makes a nutritious and delicious breakfast treat, even cold from the fridge.

LET'S BEGIN Preheat the oven to 350°F. Coat a 1½-quart baking dish with cooking spray. Cook the noodles according to package directions. Drain.

MIX IT UP Meanwhile, beat the Neufchâtel and ricotta together in a large bowl until light and fluffy. Gradually beat in the sugar until well blended. Beat in the eggs, one at a time, until blended. Gradually beat in the milk, melted butter, and ½ teaspoon cinnamon until smooth. Stir in the cooked noodles. Spoon the mixture into the baking dish, smoothing the top. Sprinkle with additional cinnamon, if you like.

INTO THE OVEN Bake for 35 to 40 minutes, until an instant-read thermometer inserted near the center reads at least 160°F and the kugel is light golden brown. Cool for 10 minutes before serving.

Makes 6 servings

Per serving: 474 calories, 16g protein, 47g carbohydrates, 25g fat, 12g saturated fat, 234mg cholesterol, 326mg sodium

SAVORY ORZO

Prep **10 MINUTES**   *Cook* **20 MINUTES**

4	cups orzo
4	slices bacon
1	cup sliced scallions
½	cup grated Parmesan cheese
½	cup pine nuts, toasted
2	teaspoons Italian seasoning
¾	teaspoon seasoned salt

Pine nuts—also known as pignoli, piñon, and Indian nuts—are flavorful nuts that come from several types of pine trees. The nuts are found inside the pine cones, which makes removing the nuts time-consuming and explains why they are also rather expensive.

LET'S BEGIN Cook the pasta according to package directions. Drain and keep warm.

INTO THE PAN Meanwhile, cook the bacon in a large skillet over medium heat until crispy. Drain on paper towels, then crumble. Sauté the scallions in the bacon drippings for 1 to 2 minutes, until crisp-tender. Stir in the orzo, bacon, ¼ cup of the cheese, the pine nuts, Italian seasoning, and seasoned salt. Cook for 1 to 2 minutes, until heated through. Top with the remaining ¼ cup cheese.

Makes 6 servings

Per serving: 400 calories, 17g protein, 56g carbohydrates, 12g fat, 2g saturated fat, 10mg cholesterol, 405mg sodium

Food Facts

ORZO—IT'S REALLY PASTA

Orzo may look like rice, but it's not. And even though its name means "barley" in Italian, it's not barley either. Orzo is actually pasta that's just shaped like rice. And like rice, it's small—a little smaller than a pine nut.

You'll often find orzo used in soups or tossed with grilled vegetables to make a delicious pasta salad. But its versatility doesn't stop there. It's often prepared risotto-style to make a delectable side dish. And in Greece, you'll often find it served with lamb.

SuperQuick

GARLIC MASHED POTATOES

Prep **10 MINUTES**   *Cook* **20 MINUTES**

6	medium all-purpose potatoes, peeled and cut into 1-inch chunks
1½	cups low-fat milk
3	tablespoons margarine
4	garlic cloves, minced
⅛	teaspoon salt
⅛	teaspoon ground black pepper

Cooking garlic in milk takes the bite out and leaves in all of the garlic's good flavor. If you prefer richer potatoes, use whole milk.

LET'S BEGIN Bring 2 inches of water to a boil in a large saucepan. Add the potatoes, cover, and cook for about 10 minutes, or until tender. Drain well. Return the potatoes to the pan and shake over low heat for 1 to 2 minutes, until dry. Mash the potatoes with a potato masher or beat with an electric handheld mixer. Cover and keep warm.

MIX & SERVE Combine the milk, margarine, and garlic in a small saucepan. Simmer over medium-low heat until heated through. Beat the hot milk mixture into the potatoes until well mixed and fluffy. (Add more milk for a creamier consistency, if desired.) Stir in the salt and pepper.

Makes 6 servings

Per serving: 196 calories, 5g protein, 30g carbohydrates, 7g fat, 2g saturated fat, 2mg cholesterol, 137mg sodium

Cooking Basics

THE EASIEST WAY TO ROAST GARLIC

Roasting a whole head of garlic is like money in the bank. Once it's roasted, the sweet, mellow garlic pulp can be used to flavor a limitless number of foods, including salad dressing, mashed potatoes, poultry stuffing, bean salads, and soups.

Here's the favorite method for roasting garlic:

• To begin: Preheat the oven or toaster oven to 350°F. Remove any papery skin from the head (or heads) of garlic, leaving the garlic intact. With a serrated knife, cut off the top ½ inch of the garlic.
• Flavor it: Place the head of garlic on a sheet of heavy-duty foil. Drizzle it with olive oil and season with salt and pepper. If you like,

sprinkle the top with a little dried thyme. Then enclose the garlic completely in the foil.
• Into the oven: Bake it for about 1 hour, or until the garlic has softened.
• When the garlic is cool enough to handle: Separate the cloves and squeeze each gently to remove the soft garlic inside.

HONEY-MUSTARD ROASTED POTATOES

Prep **20 MINUTES**   *Cook* **20 MINUTES**

4   large baking potatoes, peeled and each cut into 6 to 8 pieces

½   cup Dijon mustard

¼   cup honey

½   teaspoon dried thyme, crushed

Salt and ground black pepper

These hot-sweet potatoes go really well with pork chops, baked ham, and roasted chicken. Round out the meal with your favorite green vegetable.

LET'S BEGIN Combine the potatoes with enough salted water to cover and bring to a boil. Reduce the heat and simmer for 12 to 15 minutes, until barely tender. Drain and transfer to a large bowl.

TOSS IT Preheat the oven to 375°F. Line a large cookie sheet with foil. Spray the foil with cooking spray. Combine the mustard, honey, and thyme in a small bowl. Add the honey-mustard mixture to the hot potatoes and toss until evenly coated. Arrange the potatoes on the sheet.

INTO THE OVEN Bake for 20 minutes, or until the potatoes are tender and begin to brown around the edges. Season to taste with salt and pepper.

Makes 4 servings

Per serving: 296 calories, 6g protein, 65g carbohydrates, 2g fat, 0g saturated fat, 0mg cholesterol, 726mg sodium

EASY TWICE-BAKED POTATOES

Prep 10 MINUTES   Cook 15 MINUTES

3   large baking potatoes

½   cup sour cream

2   tablespoons butter or margarine

1⅓   cups prepared french-fried onions or Cheddar french-fried onions

1   cup shredded Cheddar cheese (4 ounces)

Everyone loves twice-baked potatoes—and for good reason. They are so-o-o delicious! Using the microwave to cook and reheat the potatoes cuts out lots of kitchen time.

LET'S BEGIN Prick the skins of the potatoes with a fork. Place in a circular pattern on a microwaveable plate. Microwave on High for 12 to 15 minutes, or until the potatoes are soft.

MIX & FILL Cut the potatoes in half lengthwise and scoop out the insides, leaving a thin shell. Transfer the potato flesh to a bowl. Mash the potatoes with the sour cream and butter until smooth. Stir in ⅔ cup of the onions and ½ cup of the cheese. Spoon the mixture into the shells.

COOK & SERVE Arrange the potato halves on a microwaveable plate. Microwave on High for 3 to 5 minutes, or until heated through. Top each with the remaining ½ cup cheese and ⅔ cup onions. Microwave 1 minute longer, or until the cheese melts.

Makes 6 servings

Per serving: 320 calories, 8g protein, 28g carbohydrates, 20g fat, 10g saturated fat, 38mg cholesterol, 271mg sodium

BEST EVER POTATOES AU GRATIN

Prep **20 MINUTES**   *Bake* **27 MINUTES**

2   tablespoons butter

3   tablespoons all-purpose flour

2   cups milk

1   teaspoon salt

½   teaspoon ground black pepper

3   large baking potatoes, boiled, peeled, and cut into ¼-inch-thick slices

8   slices deli-style medium Cheddar cheese (6 ounces, about ¾ ounce each)

Paprika (optional)

You can cook, peel, and slice the potatoes early in the day so that the dish can be put together quickly. Using presliced Cheddar is a neat way of adding cheese.

LET'S BEGIN Preheat the oven to 375°F. Coat a 2-quart baking dish with cooking spray.

MAKE IT SAUCY Melt the butter in a medium saucepan over medium heat. Stir in the flour until smooth. Cook, stirring constantly, for 1 minute. Stir in the milk, salt, and pepper. Bring to a boil, stirring frequently. Reduce the heat to low. Simmer, stirring frequently, for 1 minute, or until thickened.

LAYER & BAKE Spread ½ cup of the sauce on the bottom of the baking dish. Layer with half the potatoes, half the remaining sauce, and 4 slices of the cheese. Repeat with the remaining sauce, potatoes, and cheese. Sprinkle with paprika, if you like. Bake for 25 minutes, or until bubbly.

Makes 8 servings
Per serving: 242 calories, 11g protein, 17g carbohydrates, 15g fat, 9g saturated fat, 44mg cholesterol, 519mg sodium

CHEESY HASH BROWN CASSEROLE

Prep **10 MINUTES**   Bake **1 HOUR**

1   package (32 ounces)
     frozen hash brown
     potatoes, thawed

2   cups shredded mild
     Cheddar cheese
     (8 ounces)

1   can (10¾ ounces)
     condensed cream of
     chicken soup

¾   cup butter, melted

1   medium onion, chopped
     (½ cup)

1   teaspoon salt

Dash ground black pepper

2   cups crushed cornflakes

Ground paprika

Frozen hash brown potatoes, creamy canned soup, and preshredded cheese make this recipe a breeze to put together. Crush the cornflakes fast by putting them into a plastic bag and running a rolling pin over them.

LET'S BEGIN Preheat the oven to 325°F. Combine the potatoes, cheese, soup, ½ cup of the melted butter, the onion, salt, and pepper in a large bowl. Pour the potato mixture into a 13 × 9-inch baking dish. Top with the cornflakes and the remaining ¼ cup melted butter.

INTO THE OVEN Bake for 1 hour. Sprinkle paprika over the top and serve.

Makes 12 servings

Per serving: 281 calories, 7g protein, 20g carbohydrates, 24g fat, 13g saturated fat, 52mg cholesterol, 593mg sodium

FUN FRIES

Prep **5 MINUTES**   *Bake* **30 MINUTES**

¼   **cup grated Parmesan cheese**

1   **tablespoon vegetable oil**

1   **teaspoon Italian seasoning**

4   **medium russet potatoes, cut into ½-inch wedges**

Salt (optional)

A russet is a baking potato. It's great oven-fried because it gets very crispy on the outside and nice and creamy on the inside.

LET'S BEGIN Preheat the oven to 475°F.

TOSS Combine the cheese, oil, and seasoning in a large bowl. Add the potatoes and toss to coat with the cheese mixture. Arrange in a single layer on a large cookie sheet.

INTO THE OVEN Bake the potatoes for 30 minutes, or until golden brown, tossing once after 15 minutes. Sprinkle with salt, if you like.

Makes 4 servings

Per serving: 220 calories, 6g protein, 39g carbohydrates, 5g fat, 1g saturated fat, 5mg cholesterol, 130mg sodium

Cooking Basics

FRYING FRIED POTATOES

Whether you're deep-frying or oven-frying potatoes, reach for the russets, also known as Idahos and baking potatoes. Since they don't absorb as much oil, you'll get crispier fries.

To prepare potatoes for frying:

• Cut them into uniform strips.

• Rinse them with cold running water to remove any starch.

• For the crispiest fries, soak the potatoes for a few minutes in lightly salted cold water.

• Dry the fries carefully to prevent any spatters when you add them to the oil.

To deep-fry potatoes:

• Use a heavy skillet with high sides (or an electric skillet if you have one).

• Pour in about 1 to 1½ inches of fresh oil. Avoid used oil that you've used before, as it not only has a lower smoking point but also can give the potatoes an off flavor.

• Heat the oil to 350°F—no higher! Watch the temperature of the oil closely to keep it from reaching the smoking point, as this also can give the potatoes an off flavor.

• If you don't have a deep-fry thermometer, slip a potato stick into the oil to see if the correct frying temperature has been reached. It should stay afloat and be surrounded by bubbles. If it sinks and the oil doesn't bubble up, the oil isn't hot enough yet.

• Cook the potatoes in small batches so they brown evenly. When they turn golden, transfer them to a cookie sheet lined with paper towels. Keep them hot in a low oven while frying the rest of the potatoes. Sprinkle them with salt while piping hot, if you wish.

To bake perfect oven-fries, see the recipe above, just omit the cheese.

TOUCHDOWN 'TATERS

Prep **20 MINUTES**   *Bake* **55 MINUTES**

These potatoes can be made ahead. To reheat them, cover them with foil and bake in a 375°F oven for 20 minutes, or until heated through.

4	medium baking potatoes, pierced with a fork
6	slices bacon, cut into ½-inch pieces
¼	cup cider vinegar
¼	cup milk

Salt and ground black pepper

½	cup sliced scallions
1	teaspoon poppy seeds

Chopped fresh parsley

Applesauce and sour cream (optional)

LET'S BEGIN Preheat the oven to 400°F. Bake the potatoes for about 45 minutes, or until fork-tender. Cool. (Leave the oven on.) Meanwhile, cook the bacon in a large skillet over medium heat until crispy. Drain on paper towels. Discard all but 1 tablespoon of the bacon fat. Slice off the top third of each potato lengthwise. Scoop out the insides, leaving a thin shell. Cook the potato flesh and the vinegar in the bacon fat until the potatoes absorb the vinegar. Remove the skillet from the heat. Mash the potatoes with the milk, and add salt and pepper to taste. Stir in the bacon, scallions, and poppy seeds.

STUFF & BAKE Spoon the potato filling into the shells. Transfer the potatoes to a cookie sheet. Bake for 10 minutes, or until heated through. Sprinkle with parsley. Serve with applesauce or sour cream, if you like.

Makes 4 servings

Per serving: 210 calories, 9g protein, 29g carbohydrates, 9g fat, 3g saturated fat, 16mg cholesterol, 287mg sodium

---

On the Menu

————◆•◆————

Invite the gang over for a delicious buffet supper after the final touchdown. You'll find yourself on the winning team with everyone!

————◆•◆————

Chunky Guacamole

Red Tomato Salsa

Tortilla Chips

Oven-Fried Chicken

Touchdown 'Taters

Easy Three Bean Salad

Tomato and Red Onion Salad

Creamy Coleslaw

Jumbo Chocolate Chip Cookies

Chocolate Ice Cream

Ice-Cold Lemonade

Sparkling Water

Pitchers of Beer

SWEET POTATO SOUFFLÉ

Prep **15 MINUTES**   *Bake* **55 MINUTES**

1   can (29 ounces) sweet potato pie filling

½   cup chopped walnuts

¼   cup heavy cream

¼   teaspoon salt

3   large eggs, separated

Fresh strawberries

Think of this as a light-as-air sweet potato pie! The key to separating eggs with ease is to do the separating when the eggs are just out of the fridge, then let them come to room temperature so they will beat to their highest volume.

LET'S BEGIN Preheat the oven to 425°F.

MIX IT UP Combine the pie filling, walnuts, cream, and salt in a large bowl. Whisk in the egg yolks until blended. Beat the egg whites in a medium bowl with an electric mixer on medium-high speed until stiff. With a rubber spatula, gently fold the whites into the pie filling mixture. Spoon into a 2-quart soufflé or casserole dish. Cover with foil.

INTO THE OVEN Bake for 15 minutes. Reduce the oven temperature to 350°F and bake 40 minutes longer, or until the soufflé is set. Garnish with strawberries. Serve immediately.

Makes 8 servings

Per serving: 270 calories, 5g protein, 41g carbohydrates, 10g fat, 3g saturated fat, 90mg cholesterol, 125mg sodium

CANDIED SWEET POTATOES

Prep **15 MINUTES**   *Bake* **55 MINUTES**

½   cup packed light brown sugar

1   teaspoon pumpkin pie spice

3   pounds sweet potatoes, peeled and cut into 1-inch pieces (7 to 8 cups)

2   tablespoons orange juice

1   teaspoon vanilla extract

2   tablespoons butter or margarine, cut into pieces

Candied sweet potatoes are an all-American crowd-pleaser. We love to serve them alongside the Thanksgiving turkey and all its fixings. On busy holidays, prepare the potatoes up to 3 hours ahead and then reheat them before serving.

LET'S BEGIN Preheat the oven to 350°F. Combine the brown sugar and the pumpkin pie spice in a large bowl and stir to mix well. Add the potatoes and toss to coat. Transfer the potatoes to a 13 × 9-inch baking dish.

INTO THE OVEN Combine the orange juice and vanilla and pour evenly over the potatoes. Dot the tops of the potatoes with the butter. Cover and bake for 40 minutes. Remove from the oven and stir, then bake uncovered for 15 to 20 minutes longer, until the potatoes are tender.

Makes 10 servings

Per serving: 325 calories, 3g protein, 58g carbohydrates, 12g fat, 2g saturated fat, 13mg cholesterol, 84mg sodium

DOUBLE-BAKED SWEET POTATOES

Prep **20 MINUTES**   *Bake* **20 MINUTES**

6   **baked medium sweet potatoes, slightly cooled**

½   **cup butter or margarine, melted**

6   **tablespoons apple juice**

2   **tablespoons packed brown sugar**

½   **teaspoon ground ginger**

TOPPING

1   **cup miniature marshmallows**

⅓   **cup flaked sweetened coconut**

1   **tablespoon butter or margarine, melted**

Bake the potatoes up to 2 hours ahead and keep them warm by wrapping them up in foil, or stuff the potatoes and set them aside for up to 2 hours before putting them into the oven.

LET'S BEGIN Preheat the oven to 350°F. Cut the potatoes lengthwise in half. Scoop out the potato flesh, leaving a thin shell. Transfer the potatoes to a medium bowl and mash. Add the melted butter, apple juice, brown sugar, and ginger. Beat until fluffy.

STUFF & BAKE Spoon the potato filling into the shells. Transfer the potatoes to a large cookie sheet. To make the topping, combine all the ingredients in a small bowl. Spoon over the potatoes. Bake for 20 to 25 minutes, until heated through.

Makes 12 servings

Per serving: 170 calories, 1g protein, 20g carbohydrates, 10g total fat, 5g saturated fat, 25mg cholesterol, 100mg sodium

SPRING RISOTTO

Prep **10 MINUTES**   *Cook* **10 MINUTES**

Authentic risotto tastes great, but it usually takes a good 30 minutes of cooking time. Here the time is really cut by using rice that cooks in just 5 minutes. What a treat!

3	tablespoons butter
2	tablespoons olive oil
1	medium onion, thinly sliced
2	garlic cloves, minced
2	cups minute long-grain white rice
1	can (14½ ounces) chicken or vegetable broth, warmed
½	cup milk
1	pound asparagus, cut into 2-inch lengths
⅓	cup grated Parmesan cheese
⅛	teaspoon salt
⅛	teaspoon ground black pepper

LET'S BEGIN Melt the butter with the oil in a large deep skillet over medium heat. Add the onion and garlic and cook for 2 to 3 minutes, until softened (do not brown).

COOK IT QUICK Stir the rice into the onion mixture until well coated. Add the warm broth, milk, and asparagus. Bring to a boil over medium heat. Reduce the heat to low and simmer for 5 minutes, or until the rice and asparagus are tender. Stir in ¼ cup of the cheese, the salt, and pepper.

SERVE Sprinkle the risotto with the remaining cheese just before serving.

Makes 6 servings

Per serving: 270 calories, 9g protein, 29g carbohydrates, 13g fat, 6g saturated fat, 25mg cholesterol, 460mg sodium

---

Cook to Cook

WHAT ARE SOME TIPS FOR MAKING RISOTTO?

"I like to make risotto—that classic Italian rice dish that everyone loves for its creamy texture. Once you understand what makes a perfect risotto, you'll find yourself whipping up lots of flavorful variations often.

First, you need to *buy a short-grain rice.* My favorite one is Arborio, which you can find easily in many supermarkets and specialty food stores.

It's also very important that the liquid (usually broth) that is gradually added to the cooking rice mixture (usually about ½ cup at a time) is *kept at a gentle simmer at all times.*

Stirring constantly is also important as it brings out the starch in the rice, which in turn gives it its characteristically creamy texture.

Once the rice is al dente—that is, just cooked through with a *tiny bit of firmness in the center—it's ready to serve.* (Taste a grain of rice to check.) Bon appétit!"

FRUITED RICE PILAF

Prep **10 MINUTES**   *Cook* **18 MINUTES**

2	teaspoons olive oil
1	cup basmati or long-grain white rice
1	garlic clove, minced
1	can (14½ ounces) chicken broth
¼	teaspoon ground black pepper
½	cup dried cranberries
¼	cup sliced scallions + extra for garnish (optional)
¼	cup coarsely chopped slivered almonds

This is an ideal side dish to serve with a simple roasted chicken, grilled butterflied leg of lamb, or broiled pork chops. If you like, you can use any other favorite nut, including walnuts, pecans, or hazelnuts.

LET'S BEGIN Heat the oil in a large saucepan over medium heat. Add the rice and garlic and cook for 1 to 2 minutes, until the rice is coated with the oil and the garlic is fragrant.

SIMMER LOW Stir in the broth and the pepper. Cover and bring to a boil. Reduce the heat and simmer for 10 minutes. Stir in the cranberries. Cover and cook 7 to 10 minutes longer, until the liquid is absorbed and the rice is tender.

SERVE Fluff the rice with a fork and stir in the ¼ cup scallions and almonds. Sprinkle the top with additional scallions, if you like.

Makes 5 servings
Per serving: 191 calories, 4g protein, 34g carbohydrates, 5g fat, 1g saturated fat, 0mg cholesterol, 281mg sodium

VEGETABLE FRIED RICE

Prep **5 MINUTES**   *Cook* **31 MINUTES**

Here's how to get a tasty dinner on the table fast. On your way home, pick up some spare ribs and wonton soup.

1	tablespoon vegetable oil
1	cup long-grain white rice
1	package (1.40 ounces) chicken fried rice seasoning
2¼	cups water
2	cups broccoli florets
1	cup sliced white mushrooms
2	scallions, chopped

LET'S BEGIN Heat the oil in a large skillet over medium-high heat. Stir in the rice and sauté for 1 minute. Stir in the seasoning and the water. Bring to a boil. Reduce the heat. Cover and simmer for 20 minutes, or until the rice is tender.

STIR IT IN Add the broccoli, mushrooms, and scallions and mix well. Cover and cook 5 minutes longer, or until the broccoli is tender.

Makes 4 servings

Per serving: 255 calories, 6g protein, 46g carbohydrates, 4g fat, 1g saturated fat, 0mg cholesterol, 800mg sodium

On the Menu

Celebrate the Chinese New Year in grand style with this ample buffet offering an array of fabulous flavorful foods.

Egg Drop Soup

Spring Rolls

Vegetable Fried Rice

Broccoli with Garlic & Ginger

Cold Noodles with Peanut Sauce

Honey-Glazed Spareribs

Shrimp with Cashews

Pistachio Ice Cream

Fresh Pineapple Wedges

Pots of Steaming Jasmine Tea

BLACK BEANS 'N' RICE

Prep **5 MINUTES**   *Cook* **28 MINUTES**

1	tablespoon vegetable oil
1	medium onion, chopped (½ cup)
1	cup long-grain white rice
2	cups water
1	package (1.31 ounces) Sloppy Joe seasoning
1	can (15 ounces) black beans, rinsed and drained

Adding a packet of Sloppy Joe seasoning to the rice mixture is a fast way to flavor it up. For a change of pace, you can add one 14½-ounce can of diced tomatoes along with the seasoning and beans.

LET'S BEGIN Heat the oil in a medium saucepan over medium-high heat. Sauté the onion until tender. Add the rice and the water and bring to a boil. Reduce the heat. Cover and simmer for 20 minutes, or until the rice is tender.

STIR IT IN Stir in the seasoning and beans. Cook, stirring, until heated through.

> **Makes 6 servings**
>
> *Per serving: 221 calories, 6g protein, 40g carbohydrates, 3g fat, 0g saturated fat, 0mg cholesterol, 718mg sodium*

SuperQuick

HARVEST RICE

Prep **10 MINUTES**   *Cook* **20 MINUTES**

¾	cup vegetable broth
½	cup water
1	cup instant brown rice
1	tablespoon vegetable oil
⅓	cup thinly sliced carrots
⅔	cup chopped apple
⅓	cup chopped scallions
4	teaspoons raisins
1	teaspoon sesame seeds
Dash salt	

Instant brown rice really cuts down on the cooking time in this flavorful recipe. Use either red or green apples. It just depends on whether you prefer a sweeter or more tart flavor.

LET'S BEGIN Bring the broth and the water to a boil in a medium saucepan. Add the rice. Cover and simmer for 10 minutes, or until the rice is tender. Remove from the heat.

INTO THE PAN Heat the oil in a large skillet over medium-high heat. Add the carrots and cook, stirring, until crisp-tender. Add the apple and scallions and cook for 3 minutes. Stir in the rice, raisins, ¾ teaspoon of the sesame seeds, and the salt. Cook, stirring, until heated through. Sprinkle with the remaining ¼ teaspoon sesame seeds.

> **Makes 6 servings**
>
> *Per serving: 111 calories, 2g protein, 20g carbohydrates, 3g fat, 0g saturated fat, 0mg cholesterol, 173mg sodium*

Black Beans 'n' Rice

SuperQuick
BBQ Baked Beans

Prep **5 MINUTES**   *Microwave* **25 MINUTES**

1	large green or red bell pepper, chopped + extra for garnish (optional)
1	small onion, chopped
2	slices bacon, finely chopped
3	cans (16 ounces each) pork and beans
¾	cup barbecue sauce
¼	cup mustard
¼	cup packed brown sugar

Use your favorite barbecue sauce and baked beans in this easy and delicious side dish. It's made with ease in the microwave, but directions for cooking it the old-fashioned way—in the oven—are included.

LET'S BEGIN Place the large chopped pepper, onion, and bacon in a microwaveable 3-quart bowl. Cover loosely with waxed paper and microwave on High for 5 minutes, or until the bacon is partially cooked.

STIR IT IN Stir in the pork and beans, barbecue sauce, mustard, and brown sugar.

COOK & SERVE Microwave, uncovered, on High for 20 minutes, or until heated through and the mixture is slightly thickened, stirring twice. Top with chopped pepper, if you wish.

OVEN BAKED BEANS

Preheat the oven to 400°F. Cook the pepper, onion, and bacon in a large nonstick skillet until the bacon is crisp. Transfer to a Dutch oven. Stir in the remaining ingredients. Bake for 45 to 50 minutes, stirring occasionally.

Makes 8 servings
Per serving: 250 calories, 10g protein, 47g carbohydrates, 4g fat, 1g saturated fat, 14mg cholesterol, 1,015mg sodium

OLD-FASHIONED BEAN BAKE

Prep **15 MINUTES + SOAKING**   *Cook/Bake* **5 HOURS**

1	package (1 pound) dried navy, pea, or pinto beans, rinsed and picked over
4	cups tomato juice
2	cups packed dark brown sugar
2	tablespoons dried minced onions
2	teaspoons poultry seasoning
1	teaspoon vanilla extract
1	teaspoon prepared horseradish
½	teaspoon dry mustard
¼	teaspoon ground cloves
⅛	teaspoon ground cardamom
⅛	teaspoon ground black pepper
8	slices bacon, cut into 1-inch pieces

If you find that the beans seem a bit dry during the baking time, add a small amount of hot water.

LET'S BEGIN Soak the beans according to package directions. Drain.

MIX IT UP Preheat the oven to 300°F. Place the beans in a 3-quart casserole or bean pot. Combine the remaining ingredients in a large bowl and mix well. Pour the mixture over the beans and stir.

INTO THE OVEN Cover and bake for 5 hours, or until the beans are tender, uncovering the casserole during the last 30 minutes of baking.

Makes 10 servings

Per serving: 312 calories, 13g protein, 61g carbohydrates, 3g fat, 1g saturated fat, 4mg cholesterol, 723mg sodium

Carrots with Character, page 70

The Vegetable Garden

Go ahead . . . peek into your vegetable garden to see what's ripe and ready for picking today. If you don't have a garden, choose whatever is in season at the nearby farmers' market or supermarket. Then pick one of these quick-cooking, tasty ways to steam it, sauté it, stir-fry it, oven-fry it, bake it, mash it, or glaze it. Guaranteed, you'll have a side dish where they'll ask for seconds.

Many of these recipes use fresh veggies, while others cut down on the fixing time even more by starting with frozen varieties. So steam some ever-loving corn on the cob, roast some asparagus and tomatoes, or cream some spinach for supper tonight.

ROASTED ASPARAGUS & TOMATOES WITH ALMONDS

Prep **10 MINUTES**   *Bake* **25 MINUTES**

¾   **pound asparagus, cut into ½-inch lengths**

1   **medium tomato, seeded and cut into cubes, or ¾ cup halved grape tomatoes**

2   **tablespoons vinaigrette salad dressing**

1   **tablespoon light mayonnaise**

Salt and ground black pepper

2   **tablespoons grated Parmesan cheese**

2   **tablespoons sliced almonds**

Use either jumbo or regular asparagus in this tasty dish. The pencil-thin variety is a bit too thin for roasting. If you can't find grape tomatoes in your market, cherry tomatoes are also a good choice.

LET'S BEGIN Preheat the oven to 425°F. Combine the asparagus and tomato in a medium baking dish.

TOSS & BAKE Whisk the vinaigrette and mayonnaise together in a small bowl. Season to taste with salt and pepper. Drizzle the dressing mixture over the asparagus and tomato, then toss to combine. Sprinkle the cheese and almonds over the top. Bake for 25 to 30 minutes, until the asparagus is crisp-tender.

Makes 4 servings

Per serving: 105 calories, 4g protein, 6g carbohydrates, 8g fat, 2g saturated fat, 3mg cholesterol, 144mg sodium

---

Cooking Basics

THE FASTEST WAY TO ROAST ASPARAGUS

Roasting spears of asparagus is quick and easy—plus it gives this vegetable even more delicious flavor. Keep in mind that when vegetables are roasted, they shrink a considerable amount, so you will want to start with a little more than usual.

• To begin, preheat the oven to 450°F. For every 3 servings you will need 1 pound of regular asparagus. Snap off the woody ends.

• Now, flavor them up: Spread the asparagus in a jelly-roll pan. Drizzle them well with olive oil, rolling them around until they're coated. Season with salt and pepper.

• Roast the asparagus for about 20 minutes, or until they are tender and lightly browned. Shake the pan occasionally during the roasting to keep the asparagus browning evenly. And watch closely, as thinner spears might

take a little less time to roast. Serve while hot.

• Add a little variety if you like: Transfer the asparagus to a serving dish and top with grated Parmesan, sautéed cherry tomatoes, chopped fresh herbs, chopped hazelnuts that you've browned in butter (slivered almonds or chopped pecans work too). Or drizzle with a little fresh lemon juice or balsamic vinegar right before serving.

VANILLA BEANS AMANDINE

Prep **5 MINUTES**   Cook **15 MINUTES**

1	pound fresh green beans, trimmed, or 1 package (16 ounces) frozen green beans
2	tablespoons butter
1	tablespoon dry white wine
1½	teaspoons vanilla extract
½	teaspoon onion powder
¼	teaspoon salt
⅛	to ¼ teaspoon coarsely ground black pepper
¼	cup sliced almonds, toasted

Toast almonds by spreading them in a single layer on a cookie sheet and baking them at 350°F for 8 minutes, until fragrant.

LET'S BEGIN Bring a large saucepan of water to a boil. Add the green beans and cook over medium-high heat for 7 to 8 minutes, until tender. Drain and transfer to a large bowl. Keep warm. (For frozen green beans, cook according to package directions.)

MAKE IT SAUCY Melt the butter in a small saucepan over medium heat. Stir in the wine, vanilla, onion powder, salt, and pepper. Simmer for 2 minutes.

TOSS & SERVE Toss the butter sauce with the green beans. Top with the almonds.

Makes 6 servings

Per serving: 90 calories, 2g protein, 7g carbohydrates, 6g fat, 2g saturated fat, 11mg cholesterol, 142mg sodium

HONEY-GLAZED CARROTS

Prep **10 MINUTES**   Cook **10 MINUTES**

3	cups sliced carrots
¼	cup honey
2	tablespoons butter or margarine
2	tablespoons chopped fresh parsley
1½	teaspoons Dijon mustard (optional)

This is a side dish you will make again and again. Cooking carrots with honey and butter brings out their rich flavor and gives them an enticing sheen, while the Dijon adds just the right subtle bit of bite.

LET'S BEGIN Bring 2 inches of salted water to a boil in a large saucepan. Add the carrots and return to a boil. Reduce the heat to medium. Cover and cook for 8 to 12 minutes, until crisp-tender.

STIR & SERVE Drain the carrots and return to the saucepan. Stir in the honey, butter, parsley, and mustard, if you like. Cook, stirring, over low heat until carrots are glazed.

Makes 6 servings

Per serving: 135 calories, 1g protein, 25g carbohydrates, 4g fat, 2g saturated fat, 10mg cholesterol, 122mg sodium

GREEN BEANS & FRESH TOMATO SAUCE
Prep **10 MINUTES**   *Cook* **18 MINUTES**

1	pound ripe tomatoes
¼	cup olive oil
2	garlic cloves, minced
2	pounds green beans, trimmed

Salt and ground black pepper

1	cup loosely packed fresh basil leaves, cut into very thin strips
4	ounces goat cheese, crumbled

Peeling and seeding the tomatoes gives this dish lots of concentrated tomato flavor. The combination of green beans and tomatoes is classically Italian, but the addition of goat cheese is classic American.

LET'S BEGIN Bring a pot of water to a boil. Add the tomatoes. When the water returns to a boil, cook for about 1 minute. Drain. When the tomatoes are cool enough to handle, peel them, cut them in half, and remove the seeds. Cut the tomatoes into large chunks.

INTO THE PAN Heat the oil in a large skillet over medium heat. Sauté the garlic for 1 minute, or until golden. Add the tomatoes, increase the heat, and cook for 5 to 6 minutes. Add the beans and reduce the heat to medium. Season to taste with salt and pepper. Cover and cook, stirring occasionally, for about 6 minutes, or until the beans are tender but firm. (If the beans are too watery, uncover, increase the heat to high, and cook 5 minutes longer.)

SERVE Remove the pan from the heat. Toss the beans with the basil. Sprinkle with the cheese.

Makes 6 servings
Per serving: 230 calories, 9g protein, 15g carbohydrates, 16g fat, 6g saturated fat, 20mg cholesterol, 128mg sodium

ITALIAN VEGETABLE RAGOUT

Prep **20 MINUTES**   *Cook* **20 MINUTES**

1	tablespoon olive oil
6	ounces eggplant, chopped into ½- to ¾-inch pieces
1	small zucchini, chopped into ½- to ¾-inch pieces (about 1 cup)
1	medium tomato, chopped into ½- to ¾-inch pieces (about 1 cup)
1	cup chopped green bell pepper
1	teaspoon dried basil
½	teaspoon garlic powder
½	teaspoon fennel seeds
½	teaspoon salt
¼	cup water
¼	cup chopped fresh parsley

Here's how to turn this excellent side dish into a main dish. Buy frozen fully cooked meatballs and thaw them according to package directions. Add them to the ragout and let them cook for about 5 minutes. Serve some pasta on the side and you have a meal!

LET'S BEGIN Heat the oil in a large nonstick skillet over medium heat. Add the eggplant and zucchini and cook, stirring frequently, for 4 minutes, or until the vegetables begin to lightly brown.

SIMMER IT LOW Add the tomato, bell pepper, basil, garlic powder, fennel seeds, salt, and the water. Bring to a boil. Reduce the heat to low. Cover and cook, stirring occasionally, for 10 minutes or until the zucchini is tender.

SERVE Remove the skillet from the heat. Stir in the parsley and serve.

Makes 4 servings

Per serving: 76 calories, 2g protein, 8g carbohydrates, 4g fat, 1g saturated fat, 0mg cholesterol, 305mg sodium

LEMON-ROSEMARY BROCCOLI

Prep **10 MINUTES**   *Cook* **5 MINUTES**

1   **lemon, cut in half**

4   **sprigs fresh rosemary or
     ½ teaspoon dried**

2   **heads broccoli, cut into
     small florets**

2   **tablespoons butter, cut
     into small pieces**

Salt and ground black pepper

Lemon wedges (optional)

If you want to include the tasty broccoli stalks, peel them with a vegetable peeler or small sharp knife, then coarsely chop them.

LET'S BEGIN Fill a large pot with 1 inch of water. Squeeze the juice from the lemon halves into the water along with the rosemary. Bring the water to a boil.

COOK IT QUICK Arrange the broccoli in a steamer basket and carefully set it into the water. Cover and cook for 5 to 10 minutes, just until tender. Drain well.

SERVE Transfer the broccoli to a bowl or platter. Dot with the butter and season with salt and pepper. Serve with lemon wedges, if you like.

> *Makes 6 servings*
>
> *Per serving: 66 calories, 3g protein, 6g carbohydrates, 4g fat, 2g saturated fat, 11mg cholesterol, 106mg sodium*

CARROTS WITH CHARACTER

Prep **10 MINUTES**   *Cook* **10 MINUTES**

1   **pound carrots, peeled
     and sliced**

½   **cup dried cherries**

3   **tablespoons maple syrup**

2   **tablespoons margarine**

½   **teaspoon ground nutmeg**

¼   **teaspoon ground ginger**

If you prefer, substitute 1 package (1 pound) of whole baby-cut carrots for the sliced carrots. Did you know that baby-cut carrots are not small carrots at all but regular ones that have been cut down?

LET'S BEGIN Bring a large saucepan of water to a boil. Add the carrots. Cover and cook for 8 to 10 minutes, until tender. Drain well.

COOK IT QUICK Return the carrots to the saucepan. Add all of the remaining ingredients. Cook over medium heat, stirring occasionally, until the mixture is hot and bubbly.

> *Makes 6 servings*
>
> *Per serving: 138 calories, 1g protein, 26g carbohydrates, 4g fat, 1g saturated fat, 0mg cholesterol, 105mg sodium*

Carrots with Character

BRUSSELS SPROUTS WITH LEMON & THYME

Prep **5 MINUTES**   *Cook* **25 MINUTES**

1   **package (10 ounces) frozen Brussels sprouts**

1   **tablespoon butter**

1   **teaspoon grated lemon zest**

½   **teaspoon dried thyme**

Salt and ground black pepper

Did you know that Brussels sprouts, a member of the cabbage family, have been cultivated since the 16th century? Though they are considered a "winter vegetable," you can enjoy this recipe any time of year, as it uses frozen sprouts instead of fresh.

LET'S BEGIN Cook the Brussels sprouts in a saucepan according to package directions. Drain well.

STIR & SERVE Return the Brussels sprouts to the saucepan. Stir in the butter, lemon zest, and thyme. Season to taste with salt and pepper. Cover and let stand 2 minutes, or until the butter melts. Stir again before serving.

Makes 4 servings

Per serving: 60 calories, 3g protein, 6g carbohydrates, 3g fat, 2g saturated fat, 8mg cholesterol, 101mg sodium

Cooking Basics

A TERRIFIC WAY TO TRIM BRUSSELS SPROUTS

Brussels sprouts are available year-round, but they are at their freshest from October through January, which makes them perfect for serving during the holiday season.

TRIM OFF ENDS
With a small sharp knife, trim off the stem end.

PEEL OFF LEAVES
With your fingers, peel away any dry or yellowing leaves.

CUT INTO STEM
With the tip of the same knife, cut a shallow X in the bottom of the

stem ends. (This allows for more even cooking.)

COOK 'N' SERVE
Cook in boiling salted water until tender, then drain well. They're especially delicious when tossed with some roasted chestnuts or toasted pecans.

CHEESY CAULIFLOWER BAKE

Prep **10 MINUTES**   *Bake* **20 MINUTES**

1   **package (16 ounces) frozen cauliflowerets**

1   **cup shredded carrots**

¾   **cup shredded reduced-fat sharp Cheddar cheese**

3   **tablespoons fat-free peppercorn ranch salad dressing**

3   **scallions, thinly sliced**

With only 10 minutes of prep time, this side dish is ideal for weeknights when time and energy are in short supply. Don't worry about the scallions being raw, they cook just enough from the heat of the vegetables.

LET'S BEGIN Preheat the oven to 375°F. Coat a medium baking dish with cooking spray.

MIX & BAKE Combine the cauliflower and carrots in the baking dish. Combine the cheese and dressing in a small bowl until well blended. Spoon over the vegetable mixture. Bake for 20 minutes, or until heated through. Sprinkle with the scallions and gently stir to combine.

Makes 4 servings

Per serving: 130 calories, 8g protein, 14g carbohydrates, 5g fat, 4g saturated fat, 15mg cholesterol, 350mg sodium

BROCCOLI RED PEPPER STIR-FRY

Prep **15 MINUTES**   *Cook* **5 MINUTES**

½   tablespoon olive oil

½   tablespoon walnut oil

2   large garlic cloves, finely chopped

3   cups broccoli florets

2   tablespoons water

1   large red bell pepper, cut into short strips

1   medium onion, cut crosswise in half then lengthwise into slivers

1   tablespoon lemon juice

½   teaspoon salt

Here's a colorful side dish that takes only minutes to put together. Think like a Chinese chef: Prep the ingredients ahead, so most of the work is done.

LET'S BEGIN Heat the oils in a wok or large skillet over high heat. Add the garlic and stir-fry for 30 seconds, or just until fragrant. Add the broccoli and stir-fry for 1 to 2 minutes, until the broccoli turns bright green. Add the water, cover, and remove from the heat for 2 minutes.

TOSS & SERVE Return the wok to high heat. Add the bell pepper and onion. Stir-fry 2 to 3 minutes longer, until the vegetables are crisp-tender. Toss with the lemon juice and salt.

Makes 4 servings

Per serving: 70 calories, 2g protein, 9g carbohydrates, 4g fat, 1g saturated fat, 0mg cholesterol, 307mg sodium

CORN-ON-THE-COB WITH SEASONED BUTTERS

Prep **10 MINUTES**   *Grill* **20 MINUTES**

These butters are perfect on grilled corn, delicious over grilled salmon, steamed green beans, and grilled steak, too.

DILL BUTTER

¼	cup butter, softened
1	tablespoon each chopped fresh chives and fresh dill
1	teaspoon lemon juice

ITALIAN BUTTER

¼	cup butter, softened
1	tablespoon each chopped fresh basil and fresh oregano
¼	teaspoon garlic salt

HORSERADISH PARSLEY BUTTER

¼	cup butter, softened
1	tablespoon chopped fresh parsley
2	teaspoons prepared horseradish
¼	teaspoon salt
⅛	teaspoon ground black pepper
8	ears corn, husks and silk removed

LET'S BEGIN Choose one butter and blend all ingredients together in a small bowl. Spread about 1 tablespoon over each ear of corn, wrap in a double thickness of heavy-duty foil, and tightly seal.

FIRE UP THE GRILL Meanwhile, preheat the grill to medium. Grill the corn for 20 to 25 minutes, or until tender, turning them every 5 minutes.

Makes 8 servings

Per serving (1 tablespoon Dill Butter with 1 ear of corn): 180 calories, 4g protein, 31g carbohydrates, 7g fat, 4g saturated fat, 15mg cholesterol, 80mg sodium

On the Menu

Celebrate the Fourth of July at an old-fashioned picnic. Take out a red-checked tablecloth and your favorite picnic basket. Then get ready for some old-fashioned fun and terrific good eating with our all-American menu!

Sweet & Hot Marinated Mushrooms

Macaroni Salad

Carrot & Raisin Salad

Creamy Potato Salad

Easy Three-Bean Salad

Hamburgers & Hot Dogs

Crispy Fried Chicken

Corn-on-the-Cob with Seasoned Butters

Fudgy Brownies

Peach Cobbler

Pitchers of Minted Iced Tea

SOUTHERN COLLARD GREENS
Prep **10 MINUTES**   *Cook* **1 HOUR**

12	slices bacon, chopped
1	medium onion, chopped
2	garlic cloves, minced
3	pounds fresh collard greens, tough stems removed and cut into 1-inch-wide strips
2	cups water
1	teaspoon sugar
1	teaspoon salt
½	teaspoon red-pepper flakes

To prep the collard greens, gather them into small bunches and roll them up. Then use a large knife to cut them crosswise into strips.

LET'S BEGIN Cook the bacon in a large skillet over medium heat until crispy. Drain on paper towels. Discard all but 3 tablespoons of the bacon fat. Cook the onion and garlic in the bacon fat for about 5 minutes, or until tender.

SIMMER IT LOW Stir in all remaining ingredients. Reduce the heat to low. Simmer, stirring occasionally, for 45 to 60 minutes, until the greens are tender. Stir in the bacon.

Makes 12 servings
Per serving: 100 calories, 5g protein, 8g carbohydrates, 7g fat, 3g saturated fat, 10mg cholesterol, 360mg sodium

SWEET & HOT MARINATED MUSHROOMS

Prep **15 MINUTES** *Cook* **6 MINUTES + MARINATING**

⅓   **cup honey**

¼   **cup white wine vinegar**

¼   **cup dry white wine**

2   **tablespoons vegetable oil**

1   **tablespoon soy sauce**

1   **tablespoon dark sesame oil**

1   **garlic clove, minced**

1   **scallion, chopped**

1   **teaspoon grated peeled fresh ginger**

½   **teaspoon grated orange zest**

¼   **teaspoon cayenne pepper**

1   **pound small white mushrooms**

Parsley sprigs or orange wedges

Marinated mushrooms make a great side dish to simply prepared meats and leftover roast beef or roast chicken. Or serve the mushrooms as part of an antipasto platter.

LET'S BEGIN Combine all the ingredients except the mushrooms and parsley in a medium saucepan. Cook, stirring, over low heat until the mixture is well blended and heated through.

MARINATE & SERVE Place the mushrooms in a large heatproof bowl. Pour the hot marinade over the mushrooms. Cover and marinate at room temperature, stirring occasionally, for 2 hours. Arrange the mushrooms in a serving dish. Garnish with the parsley or orange wedges.

Makes 6 servings
Per serving: 150 calories, 3g protein, 18g carbohydrates, 8g fat, 1g saturated fat, 0mg cholesterol, 215mg sodium

SQUASH BAKE

Prep **10 MINUTES** *Bake* **45 MINUTES**

2	**acorn squash, cut lengthwise in half and seeded**
¼	**cup butter or margarine**
½	**cup dried cherries**
¼	**cup chopped pecans**
3	**tablespoons packed light brown sugar**
½	**teaspoon ground cinnamon**

Acorn squash, one of the winter squashes, can be a bit challenging to cut in half. The easiest way is to use a serrated or electric knife.

LET'S BEGIN Preheat the oven to 350°F. Place the squash cut side down in a baking pan. Add enough water to just cover the bottom. Bake for 45 to 50 minutes, until fork-tender.

MAKE FILLING Meanwhile, melt the butter in a small saucepan. Add the cherries, pecans, brown sugar, and cinnamon. Fill the center of each squash half with one-quarter of the filling. Mix some of the cooked squash with the filling and serve immediately.

Makes 4 servings

Per serving: 350 calories, 3g protein, 52g carbohydrates, 17g fat, 7g saturated fat, 32mg cholesterol, 108mg sodium

Microwave in Minutes

COOK SQUASH IN LESS THAN 10 MINUTES!

To cook squash in the microwave, halve and place, cut-side down, in a microwaveable dish. Add enough water to just cover the bottom. Microwave on High for 5 to 7 minutes, or until fork-tender.

ACORN SQUASH

Prep **15 MINUTES**   *Bake* **1 HOUR**

2   **medium acorn squash, pierced with a fork**

2   **oranges, peeled and cut into sections**

3   **tablespoons butter or margarine, melted**

3   **tablespoons maple syrup**

¼   **teaspoon freshly grated nutmeg**

Salt and ground black pepper

Take advantage of the look and taste of acorn squash, one of the harbingers of fall. When buying oranges, look for firm skin without any wrinkles and fruit that is heavy for its size, which indicates lots of flavorful juice.

LET'S BEGIN Preheat the oven to 375°F. Bake the squash for 1 to 1½ hours, until tender when pierced with a knife.

STUFF & SEASON Cut each squash in half lengthwise and remove the seeds. Arrange the squash halves cut side up in a dish. Fill the centers with the orange sections, then drizzle with the melted butter and maple syrup. Sprinkle the nutmeg over each squash half and season with salt and pepper.

Makes 4 servings

Per serving: 238 calories, 2g protein, 40g carbohydrates, 10g total fat, 5g saturated fat, 24mg cholesterol, 145mg sodium

Cooking Basics

THE EASIEST WAY TO PREPARE WINTER SQUASH

Here's how to get winter squash ready for cooking:

With a large knife, cut the squash lengthwise in half. It is not easy to cut through and the skin is slippery, so hold the squash firmly as you cut.

With a metal spoon, scrape out the seeds and stringy portion from both halves.

Preheat the oven to 350°F. Pour ¼ inch of water into a baking dish and place the squash cut side down in the dish. Bake for 45 to 60 minutes, until tender when pierced

with the tip of a knife. If you wish, turn them over and drizzle the center with melted butter, sweeten with brown sugar or maple syrup, and sprinkle with a little cinnamon. Return to the oven a few minutes until bubbling hot.

PEAS WITH PIZZAZZ

Prep **10 MINUTES**   *Cook* **6 MINUTES**

1	chicken bouillon cube
3	tablespoons hot tap water
3	tablespoons butter or margarine
¼	cup minced scallions
1	package (10 ounces) frozen peas
1	tablespoon minced fresh parsley
2	teaspoons honey
1	cup chopped Boston or butter lettuce

Frozen peas are a great vegetable. They are easy to use and are very often more tender than the fresh peas available in the produce section. Just be sure to use them while frozen.

LET'S BEGIN Dissolve the bouillon cube in the water and set aside. Melt the butter in a medium saucepan over medium heat. Sauté the scallions for about 2 minutes, or until tender.

SIMMER IT LOW Add the peas, parsley, and honey. Reduce the heat to low. Cover and simmer for 2 to 3 minutes. Add the lettuce and bouillon to the pan. Cover and simmer 2 to 3 minutes longer, until the peas are tender.

Makes 4 servings

Per serving: 152 calories, 4g protein, 14g carbohydrates, 9g fat, 5g saturated fat, 24mg cholesterol, 394mg sodium

SPEEDY CREAMED SPINACH

Prep **5 MINUTES**   *Cook* **7 MINUTES**

2	packages (10 ounces each) frozen chopped spinach, thawed
4	ounces cream cheese or reduced-fat cream cheese, cut into small pieces
½	teaspoon garlic salt
¼	teaspoon onion powder
⅛	to ¼ teaspoon ground nutmeg
2	tablespoons butter

Reserving and using the liquid left from thawing the spinach is a clever way to use the tasty and vitamin-filled liquid.

LET'S BEGIN Squeeze the thawed spinach and reserve the liquid. Add enough water to the liquid to equal ¾ cup.

COOK IT QUICK Heat a 12-inch skillet over medium heat until hot. Add all the remaining ingredients except the butter. Whisk for about 2 minutes, or until the cream cheese melts and is completely smooth. Stir in the spinach until well blended. Cook, stirring occasionally, for 3 minutes, or until heated through. Add the butter and cook 1 minute longer, or until the butter melts.

Makes 6 servings

Per serving: 133 calories, 5g protein, 6g carbohydrates, 11g fat, 6g saturated fat, 32mg cholesterol, 300mg sodium

SWEET AND SOUR ZUCCHINI

Prep **15 MINUTES + CHILLING**

4	**medium zucchini, thinly sliced (about 7 cups)**
½	**cup honey**
½	**cup white wine vinegar**
⅓	**cup vegetable oil**
¼	**cup chopped green bell pepper**
¼	**cup diced celery**
1	**tablespoon chopped onion**
1	**teaspoon salt**
1	**teaspoon ground black pepper**

This is a great recipe for all the home gardeners who are faced with way too many zucchini in August and September. Save time here by slicing the zucchini with a vegetable slicer or in a food processor.

LET'S BEGIN Combine all the ingredients in a large glass or ceramic bowl.

CHILL & SERVE Cover and refrigerate overnight. Drain and serve chilled or at room temperature.

Makes 8 cups

Per cup: 167 calories, 1g protein, 21g carbohydrates, 9g fat, 1g saturated fat, 0mg cholesterol, 306mg sodium

GREEK-STYLE VEGETABLES

Prep **20 MINUTES + MARINATING**   *Cook* **20 MINUTES**

1   large head cauliflower, cut into florets

1   medium zucchini, sliced into thin rounds

1   medium red onion, halved and thinly sliced

1½   cups dry white wine

¾   cup distilled white vinegar

⅓   cup olive oil

2   bay leaves

6   whole black peppercorns

1¼   teaspoons salt

1   tablespoon chopped fresh basil or 1 teaspoon dried

2   teaspoons chopped fresh thyme or 1 teaspoon dried

3   large tomatoes, halved, seeded, and diced

¼   cup chopped fresh parsley

When choosing cauliflower, look for a creamy white head without any soft spots or black marks. When you get it home, place it in the crisper drawer of the refrigerator.

LET'S BEGIN Combine the first 6 ingredients in a large nonreactive pot. Add just enough water to cover the vegetables. Stir in the next 5 ingredients.

SIMMER LOW Bring the liquid to a boil. Reduce the heat and simmer, partially covered, for about 15 minutes, or until the cauliflower is just crisp-tender.

CHILL & SERVE Transfer the vegetables and liquid to a glass or ceramic bowl. Cool. Cover and refrigerate overnight. Drain the vegetables (the liquid can be used to cook another batch of vegetables) and transfer to a large bowl. Add the tomatoes and parsley and toss to mix well. Serve cold or at room temperature.

Makes 6 servings

Per serving: 90 calories, 5g protein, 11g carbohydrates, 3g fat, 0g saturated fat, 0mg cholesterol, 170mg sodium

Tomatoes Stuffed with Couscous, page 102

Substantial Sides

Some sides are too delicious to be served only on weekdays—they deserve to be shared. For instance, that family favorite Traditional Macaroni & Cheese makes the perfect dish to take to the fundraising supper at school. To celebrate the harvest of corn, nothing's better than Corn Pudding and grilled pork chops for a Sunday family gathering. The Cheddar-Stuffed Spuds are ideal for your Fourth of July patio party. And when the end of the year rolls around, here's where you'll find a lucky Pot of Black-Eyed Peas to simmer up for New Year's Day. You'll fast discover that these sides are not only great for these celebrations, but for everyday suppers too.

TRADITIONAL MACARONI & CHEESE

Prep **15 MINUTES** Bake **25 MINUTES**

Classic-style mac and cheese is always a welcome side dish. Evaporated milk gives it lots of richness, while 2 cups of sharp Cheddar make it ever so cheesy.

1⅔ cups small elbow macaroni

2 tablespoons cornstarch

1 teaspoon salt

½ teaspoon dry mustard

¼ teaspoon ground black pepper

1 can (12 ounces) evaporated milk

2 tablespoons butter or margarine

1 cup water

2 cups shredded sharp Cheddar cheese (8 ounces)

LET'S BEGIN Cook the macaroni according to package directions. Drain and keep warm.

MIX IT UP Preheat the oven to 375°F. Grease a 2-quart casserole dish. Combine the cornstarch, salt, mustard, and pepper in a medium saucepan. Stir in the evaporated milk, butter, and the water. Cook over medium heat, stirring constantly, until the mixture comes to a boil. Boil for 1 minute. Remove from the heat. Stir in 1½ cups of the cheese until melted. Add the pasta and mix well.

INTO THE OVEN Pour into the casserole dish. Top with the remaining ½ cup cheese. Bake for 20 to 25 minutes, until the cheese melts and is lightly browned.

Makes 6 servings

Per serving: 393 calories, 17g protein, 32g carbohydrates, 21g fat, 13g saturated fat, 67mg cholesterol, 714mg sodium

BROILED GRITS WEDGES

Prep **10 MINUTES + CHILLING**   *Cook* **13 MINUTES + CHILLING**

¾   **cup grits**

½   **teaspoon salt**

3   **cups boiling water**

½   **cup shredded sharp Cheddar cheese**

2   **tablespoons chopped scallions**

½   **teaspoon mustard**

Southerners adore grits—plain, with cheese, and even with garlic. These grits are made really easy, since they are spread in a pie plate and refrigerated until you are ready to cut them into wedges and cook. Broil them until they're crisp and tempting.

LET'S BEGIN Lightly coat a 9- or 10-inch pie plate with cooking spray. Gradually stir the grits and salt into the boiling water in a medium saucepan. Reduce the heat to medium-low, cover, and cook for 5 to 7 minutes, stirring occasionally. Remove the pan from the heat. Stir in the cheese, scallions, and mustard until the cheese melts. Pour the grits mixture into the pie plate. Cover and refrigerate for about 1 hour, or until firm.

BROIL Preheat the broiler to high. Lightly coat a baking pan with cooking spray. Cut the grits into 8 wedges. Arrange the wedges on the pan. Broil the wedges for 8 to 10 minutes, or until golden brown.

Makes 8 servings

Per serving: 87 calories, 3g protein, 13g carbohydrates, 3g fat, 2g saturated fat, 7mg cholesterol, 196mg sodium

Cooking Basics

RISOTTO SIMPLIFIED

Nothing is quite as rewarding as the rich, creamy flavor of risotto cooked to perfection. It takes time and care to accomplish this goal, but the process is really very simple.

PICK THE RIGHT RICE
Arborio, a short-grain rice is used to make the risotto.

CHOOSE THE PROPER POT
A large heavy pot or saucepan that heats evenly over the bottom is the best.

STIR AND STIR SOME MORE
Sauté a finely chopped small onion in 2 tablespoons of butter until translucent, about 5 minutes.

• Add the rice (2 cups will serve 6) and cook, stirring, until it turns opaque and pearl-like, about 3 minutes. Add dry white wine (½ to 1 cup) and cook, stirring, until it evaporates.

• Add the chicken broth (6 to 8 cups total) ½ cup at a time, stirring constantly. When the broth is fully absorbed, add more.

• Continue adding broth until the rice is cooked. Stir in grated Parmesan cheese to taste.

SEAFOOD RISOTTO

Prep **20 MINUTES**   *Cook* **27 MINUTES**

6   to 8 cups seafood stock or chicken broth

4   tablespoons butter or margarine

1   medium onion, chopped

Salt and ground black pepper

2   cups Arborio rice

1   teaspoon chopped garlic

1   pound white fish fillets

½   pound medium shrimp, peeled and deveined

½   pound kielbasa or other smoked sausage, thinly sliced

½   cup grated Parmesan cheese + additional for garnish (optional)

¼   cup heavy cream

3   tablespoons chopped scallions (green part only)

2   tablespoons finely chopped fresh parsley

Short-grain rice, such as Arborio, makes the best risotto. It produces the creamiest results possible due to its very starchy nature. Look for the word Superfino *on the label. It tells you that the grains are the largest—and therefore the best.*

LET'S BEGIN Bring the stock to a boil in a medium saucepan. Reduce the heat and keep the stock at a low boil. Meanwhile, melt 3 tablespoons of the butter in a large skillet over medium-high heat. Sauté the onion until it softens but does not turn brown. Season the onion with the salt and pepper. Add the rice and garlic and cook until the rice begins to turn opaque. Gradually add 6 cups of the hot stock, 1 cup at a time, stirring constantly, until the liquid is absorbed after each addition, for 16 minutes.

SIMMER & STIR Add the fish to the rice and cook for 3 minutes, stirring to break up the fish into smaller pieces. Stir in the shrimp, sausage, and some of the remaining 2 cups stock, if necessary, to keep the rice creamy and moist. Cook for 2 minutes, or until the shrimp turn pink. Add the ½ cup Parmesan, cream, scallions, and the remaining 1 tablespoon butter and cook 2 minutes longer. Season with the salt and pepper.

SERVE Spoon the risotto into 4 serving bowls. Sprinkle with the parsley and more Parmesan cheese, if you like, and serve immediately.

Makes 4 servings

Per serving: 890 calories, 53g protein, 84g carbohydrates, 40g fat, 17g saturated fat, 238mg cholesterol, 2,546mg sodium

"I usually begin with a **1-pound loaf of firm white bread** that I cut into cubes and let dry slightly. I then sauté **2 large onions, chopped, 2 ribs of celery, chopped, and about 1 cup of chopped carrots in 1 stick of butter until tender.** I season it well with salt and pepper.

Sometimes I like to cook some **thick-sliced bacon (about ½ pound),** then crumble it and add it to the stuffing mixture along **with about 1 teaspoon caraway seeds, 2 tart apples, chopped, and a pound of bagged sauerkraut.**

Around the holidays, I add about **2 cups of fresh cranberries, about ½ pound of sweet Italian sausage links that I've cooked and crumbled, and a generous handful of chopped and toasted pecans** to the basic stuffing mixture. Absolutely delicious!"

HERBED BREAD STUFFING

Prep **15 MINUTES**   *Cook/Bake* **55 MINUTES**

This makes a super side dish for grilled boneless, skinless chicken breasts or a deli roast chicken that you simply reheat to serve.

6   tablespoons butter or margarine

1½   cups chopped onion

1   cup finely chopped celery

1   large carrot, shredded (about ½ cup)

1   large garlic clove, minced

¾   cup dry white wine

1   tablespoon each chopped fresh sage, fresh thyme, and fresh rosemary

10   cups cubed French bread (sliced ¾ inch)

1   can (14½ ounces) chicken broth

1   teaspoon seasoned salt

¼   teaspoon ground black pepper

1   large egg, beaten

LET'S BEGIN Preheat the oven to 350°F. Grease a 13 × 9-inch baking dish. Melt the butter in a large skillet over medium-high heat. Sauté the onion, celery, carrot, and garlic for 5 minutes, or until the carrot is crisp-tender. Add the wine and cook for 2 minutes. Add the herbs and sauté for 1 minute longer.

MIX & BAKE Place the bread cubes in a large bowl. Stir in the vegetable mixture, broth, seasoned salt, and pepper. Adjust the seasoning, if you wish. Blend in the egg and spoon into the baking dish. Cover and bake for 30 minutes. Uncover and bake 15 minutes longer, or until the top is crisp and golden.

Makes 8 servings

Per serving: 263 calories, 6g protein, 32g carbohydrates, 12g fat, 5g saturated fat, 51mg cholesterol, 844mg sodium

MEXICAN MINI QUICHES

Prep **10 MINUTES**   *Bake* **25 MINUTES**

1½ **cups reduced-fat shredded Mexican four-cheese blend (6 ounces)**

1 **cup egg substitute**

1 **cup seasoned croutons, crushed**

⅓ **cup chunky salsa**

¼ **cup nonfat milk**

¼ **teaspoon ground cumin**

¼ **teaspoon garlic powder**

1 **teaspoon dried cilantro (optional)**

Quiche also makes a great appetizer. Here's how: Prepare the quiche mixture as directed. Pour it into a greased 8-inch square baking dish. Bake at 375°F for 25 minutes, or until set. Cut the quiche into squares to serve.

LET'S BEGIN Preheat the oven to 375°F. Coat 24 mini muffin pan cups with cooking spray.

MIX IT UP Combine all the ingredients, including the cilantro, if you like, in a large bowl. Mix until well blended.

INTO THE OVEN Fill the muffin cups with the quiche mixture (do not overfill). Bake for 25 minutes, or until set and lightly browned. Cool the quiches in the pans for 5 minutes. Unmold onto wire racks and serve warm.

Makes 24 servings

Per serving: 37 calories, 3g protein, 2g carbohydrates, 2g fat, 1g saturated fat, 5mg cholesterol, 111mg sodium

CORN PUDDING

Prep **20 MINUTES**   *Bake* **1 HOUR**

2	cans (14.75 ounces each) cream-style corn
1	can (11 ounces) whole-kernel corn, drained
4	large eggs, well beaten
⅓	cup sugar
3	tablespoons cornstarch
1	tablespoon dried minced onions
1½	teaspoons seasoned salt
½	teaspoon dry mustard
½	cup milk
¼	cup butter or margarine, melted

Corn pudding has been enjoyed in America since the colonists, and its popularity is not about to wane anytime soon. For a change of pace, you can sprinkle the top of the pudding with shredded Cheddar about 5 minutes before the pudding is done baking.

LET'S BEGIN Preheat the oven to 350°F. Grease a 3-quart baking dish.

MIX & BLEND Combine all the corn and the eggs in a large bowl. Add the sugar, cornstarch, minced onions, seasoned salt, and mustard. Stir in the milk and melted butter.

INTO THE OVEN Pour the mixture into the baking dish. Bake for 1 hour, stirring once.

Makes 12 servings

Per serving: 208 calories, 5g protein, 29g carbohydrates, 8g fat, 2g saturated fat, 98mg cholesterol, 583mg sodium

SuperQuick
GRILLED PORTOBELLO MUSHROOMS

Prep **5 MINUTES + MARINATING**   *Grill* **5 MINUTES**

¼	cup olive oil
2	tablespoons steak seasoning
¼	cup water
6	ounces sliced portobello mushrooms

If you love the meaty, earthy flavor of grilled portobello mushrooms, use them to top hamburgers or strip steaks, or pile them onto grilled slices of country bread that you've drizzled with olive oil and rubbed with garlic. Fabulous!

LET'S BEGIN Combine the oil, seasoning, and ¼ cup water in a large resealable plastic bag. Add the mushrooms. Press out the air and seal the bag. Marinate at least 15 minutes.

FIRE UP THE GRILL Preheat the grill to medium. Grill the mushrooms for about 5 minutes, or just until tender.

Makes 4 servings

Per serving: 88 calories, 1g protein, 3g carbohydrates, 7g fat, 1g saturated fat, 0mg cholesterol, 482mg sodium

HOLIDAY YAMS & PECANS

Prep **15 MINUTES**   *Bake* **30 MINUTES**

If you like, bake this casserole in your favorite oven-proof dish, especially if you plan on bringing the casserole directly to the dining table. Canned yams not only taste great but also cut out lots of kitchen time.

3	cups canned yams, drained and mashed
1	cup granulated sugar
2	large eggs
½	cup milk
½	cup melted butter
1	teaspoon vanilla extract

TOPPING

1	cup packed brown sugar
⅓	cup self-rising flour
⅓	cup melted butter
1	cup chopped pecans

LET'S BEGIN Preheat the oven to 350°F. Grease a 13 × 9-inch baking pan.

MIX IT UP Whisk the yams, granulated sugar, eggs, milk, ½ cup melted butter, and vanilla together in a large bowl until blended. Pour into the baking pan.

TOP & BAKE To make the topping, combine the brown sugar, flour, and ⅓ cup melted butter in a medium bowl. Sprinkle the topping over the yam mixture, then sprinkle the pecans on top. Bake for 30 minutes, or until heated through.

Makes 8 servings

Per serving: 595 calories, 5g protein, 76g carbohydrates, 32g fat, 12g saturated fat, 108mg cholesterol, 272mg sodium

CHEESY STUFFED MUSHROOMS

Prep **35 MINUTES**   *Bake* **15 MINUTES**

12	large white mushrooms
1	tablespoon olive oil
½	cup finely chopped onion
⅓	cup dry white wine
1	tablespoon minced fresh parsley
½	teaspoon dried basil
1	cup shredded mozzarella cheese (4 ounces)
¼	cup grated Parmesan cheese

Sometimes very large white mushrooms are labeled "stuffing mushrooms." Make sure they are nice and white, without any wrinkling or browning.

LET'S BEGIN Preheat the oven to 350°F. Remove the stems from the mushrooms and set the caps aside. Coarsely chop the stems.

INTO THE PAN Heat the oil in a large nonstick skillet over medium-low heat. Add the chopped mushroom stems and the onion. Cook for 5 minutes, or until tender. Stir in the wine, parsley, and basil. Simmer for 10 minutes, or until the wine is absorbed. Remove the skillet from the heat and cool for 5 minutes. Stir in the mozzarella and Parmesan cheeses.

STUFF & BAKE Fill the mushroom caps with the cheese mixture and place in an 8-inch square baking pan. Bake the mushrooms for 15 minutes, or until the filling is hot and the cheese is melted.

Makes 6 servings

Per serving: 124 calories, 8g protein, 5g carbohydrates, 8g fat, 4g saturated fat, 16mg cholesterol, 210mg sodium

TOMATO AND POTATO CASSEROLE

Prep **20 MINUTES**   *Bake* **1 ¼ HOURS**

½   **cup grated Parmesan cheese**

2   **tablespoons semolina or cornmeal**

2   **tablespoons chopped fresh oregano or 2 teaspoons dried**

4   **large tomatoes, cut into ⅛-inch-thick slices**

Salt and ground black pepper

6 to 8 medium all-purpose potatoes, peeled and very thinly sliced

1   **small onion, finely chopped**

This classic Italian and very flavorful side dish can be baked up to 3 hours ahead. Then when you are ready to serve it, put it into the oven for about 20 minutes, or until heated through. In fact, it tastes even better when the flavors have had a chance to meld.

LET'S BEGIN Preheat the oven to 400°F. Grease a deep 10-inch round casserole or gratin dish. Combine the cheese, semolina, and oregano in a small bowl.

LAYER IT EASY Put a layer of about ⅓ of the tomatoes on the bottom of the casserole. Lightly sprinkle with salt and pepper, then sprinkle with about 2 tablespoons of the cheese mixture. Top with a layer of ½ of the potato slices, over-lapping slightly. Sprinkle lightly with salt, pepper, and ½ of the onion. Repeat the layers. Top with the remaining tomatoes and cheese mixture.

INTO THE OVEN Cover with foil and bake for 1¼ to 1½ hours, or until the potatoes are tender. Uncover and let stand for 5 minutes before serving.

Makes 4 servings

Per serving: 240 calories, 10g protein, 45g carbohydrates, 3g fat, 2g saturated fat, 9mg cholesterol, 245mg sodium

POT OF BLACK-EYED PEAS

Prep **5 MINUTES + SOAKING**   *Cook* **1 HOUR 15 MINUTES**

1	package (1 pound) dried black-eyed peas, picked over and rinsed
4	slices reduced-sodium bacon, cut into pieces
½	teaspoon red-pepper flakes
4	cups water
½	teaspoon salt
1	tablespoon all-purpose flour

Eat like a Southerner and enjoy a generous helping of these flavorful black-eyed peas!

LET'S BEGIN Soak the peas according to package directions. Drain. Cook the bacon and pepper flakes in a large saucepan over medium heat until crispy. Discard all but 1 tablespoon of the bacon fat. Add the soaked peas, water, and salt. Bring to a boil. Reduce the heat to low. Simmer, partially covered, for 1 hour, or until the peas are tender, stirring occasionally.

PUREE & SERVE Purée 2 cups of the peas with the pot liquid and the flour in a blender. Return the purée to the saucepan. Simmer, stirring occasionally, until slightly thickened.

Makes 16 servings

Per serving: 110 calories, 7g protein, 17g carbohydrates, 2g fat, 1g saturated fat, 5mg cholesterol, 95mg sodium

SuperQuick
CHEESE DIPPED VEGGIES

Prep **10 MINUTES**

1½	cups shredded Cheddar-Jack cheese (6 ounces)
½	cup ranch, French, or Thousand Island salad dressing
Ground paprika (optional)	
8	each: baby carrots, celery sticks, breadsticks, cherry tomatoes, and apple wedges

Make dipping veggies a real social event with this scrumptious recipe!

LET'S BEGIN Combine ½ cup of the cheese and the dressing in a bowl. Transfer to 4 custard cups. Sprinkle with paprika, if you like. Divide the remaining 1 cup cheese among 4 more custard cups.

TO SERVE On each of 4 plates, place a cup with the dressing mixture and a cup with the cheese, centering the cups on the plates. Arrange the carrots, celery, breadsticks, tomatoes, and apples on the plates. Dip each item first in the dressing mixture, then in the cheese.

Makes 4 servings

Per serving: 537 calories, 14g protein, 67g carbohydrates, 27g fat, 10g saturated fat, 52mg cholesterol, 612mg sodium

CHEDDAR-STUFFED SPUDS

Prep **35 MINUTES**   *Bake* **1 HOUR 15 MINUTES**

4	large baking potatoes
4	slices bacon, cut into pieces
2	cups small broccoli florets
½	cup chopped onion
1½	cups shredded sharp Cheddar cheese (6 ounces)
½	teaspoon salt
¼	teaspoon ground black pepper
	Salsa or sour cream (optional)

You can also use your microwave to cook these delicious potatoes!

LET'S BEGIN Preheat the oven to 400°F. Bake the potatoes for 55 minutes, or until fork-tender. Cool for 10 minutes.

MAKE FILLING Meanwhile, cook the bacon in a large skillet until crispy. Drain on paper towels. Discard all but 1 tablespoon of the bacon fat. Cook the broccoli and onions in the bacon fat over medium-high heat, stirring occasionally, for 8 to 10 minutes, until tender. Slice off the top fourth of each potato lengthwise. Scoop out the inside of the potatoes leaving a thin shell. Stir the potato flesh, 1 cup of the cheese, the salt, pepper, and the bacon into the vegetable mixture.

STUFF & BAKE Place the shells in a 2-quart baking dish. Spoon the potato filling into the shells. Top with the remaining ½ cup cheese. Bake for 20 minutes, or until heated through. Serve with salsa or sour cream, if you like.

Makes 4 servings

Per serving: 383 calories, 18g protein, 38g carbohydrates, 18g fat, 10g saturated fat, 51mg cholesterol, 709mg sodium

Microwave in Minutes

CUT POTATO BAKING TIME BY ONE-THIRD

Make these Cheddar-Stuffed Spuds in about one-third the time by using your microwave. Here's how:

• Prick the skins of the 4 potatoes several times, then place in a circular pattern in your microwave. Cook the potatoes according to the manufacturer's directions (for 4 potatoes, this usually takes about 9 to 12 minutes on High).

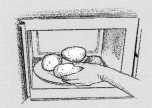

• Remove from the oven, wrap in a kitchen towel, and let stand 5 minutes.

• Scoop out the potatoes, stuff according to the recipe, and place on a microwaveable round plate.

• Loosely cover the stuffed potatoes with waxed paper. Microwave on High for 9 minutes, or until heated through, rotating the dish after 5 minutes if your oven doesn't have a turntable.

Spinach Pie

Prep **10 MINUTES**   *Bake* **36 MINUTES**

1   (9-inch) unbaked
    piecrust

2   packages (10 ounces
    each) frozen chopped
    spinach, thawed and
    squeezed dry

1   container (8 ounces)
    sour cream

⅓   cup grated Parmesan
    cheese

¼   cup seasoned dry bread
    crumbs

1   large egg

¾   teaspoon dried basil

1⅓ cups prepared french-
    fried onions

½   cup shredded mozzarella
    cheese

Prepared marinara sauce,
    heated

Spinach pie, a classic dish in Greece, gets easier and even more delicious when a prepared piecrust is used instead of phyllo dough. Save even more time by using already shredded mozzarella and pre-grated Parmesan.

LET'S BEGIN Preheat the oven to 400°F. Place the piecrust on a baking sheet.

MAKE FILLING Combine the spinach, sour cream, Parmesan, bread crumbs, egg, basil, and 1 cup of the onions in a large bowl and mix until thoroughly blended. Spread the filling in the piecrust.

INTO THE OVEN Bake for 35 minutes, or until the filling is set and the crust is browned. Sprinkle the center of the pie with the mozzarella cheese and the remaining ⅓ cup onions. Bake 1 minute longer, or until the onions are golden. Cut the pie into wedges and serve with the marinara sauce.

Makes 6 servings
Per serving: 443 calories, 13g protein, 32g carbohydrates, 30g fat, 12g saturated fat, 63mg cholesterol, 793mg sodium

STUFFED ACORN SQUASH RINGS

Prep **10 MINUTES**   *Bake* **35 MINUTES**

2   small acorn squash, cut crosswise into 1-inch-thick slices

¼   cup + 2 tablespoons butter or margarine

1   can (8 ounces) crushed pineapple

1   package (6 ounces) cornbread stuffing mix

½   cup pecan pieces, toasted

½   cup raisins

¼   cup sliced scallions

½   teaspoon ground black pepper

To save on cleanup, line the jelly-roll pan with heavy-duty foil or the new nonstick foil. You can use dried cranberries and walnuts instead of the raisins and pecans for an easy variation.

LET'S BEGIN Preheat the oven to 375°F. Arrange the squash slices in a single layer in a jelly-roll pan. Melt 2 tablespoons of the butter and brush onto the squash slices. Cover with foil and bake for 15 minutes.

MIX IT UP Meanwhile, cut the remaining ¼ cup butter into small pieces and place in a medium bowl. Drain the pineapple and reserve the juice. Add enough hot water to the pineapple juice to equal 1½ cups. Add the juice mixture to the butter and stir until the butter is melted.

STUFF & BAKE Add the pineapple, stuffing mix, pecans, raisins, scallions, and pepper. Stir just until the mixture is moistened. Spoon evenly over the hot squash slices. Bake 20 minutes longer, or until the squash is tender and the stuffing is heated through.

Makes 8 servings

Per serving: 290 calories, 4g protein, 38g carbohydrates, 15g fat, 5g saturated fat, 25mg cholesterol, 440mg sodium

TOMATOES STUFFED WITH COUSCOUS
Prep **25 MINUTES**   *Cook* **5 MINUTES**

1	cup couscous
6	large tomatoes
Salt	
1	tablespoon olive oil
¼	teaspoon hot-pepper sauce
1	garlic clove, minced

FILLING

6	scallions, finely chopped
1	cup finely chopped fresh flat-leaf parsley
⅓	cup finely chopped fresh mint
¼	cup each finely chopped green, orange, and red bell pepper
¼	cup lemon juice
3	tablespoons olive oil

Salt and ground black pepper

Parsley sprigs (optional)

Couscous, a staple of North African cuisine, cooks quickly, which makes it ideal for weeknights when time is short, and its small size makes it perfect for stuffing into vegetables.

LET'S BEGIN Prepare the couscous according to package directions. Fluff with a fork, then refrigerate until cool. Meanwhile, slice ½ inch off the top of each tomato. Discard the seeds. Remove the pulp with a spoon and chop it into small pieces. Set aside. Lightly sprinkle the tomato shells with salt. Place them upside down on a cookie sheet for about 10 minutes to drain. Combine the oil, hot-pepper sauce, and garlic. Turn the tomato shells upright and drizzle with the oil mixture.

TOSS & STUFF To make the filling, combine the scallions, parsley, mint, bell peppers, and the chilled couscous. Add the lemon juice, oil, and reserved chopped tomato. Toss and season with salt and pepper. Cut a thin slice off the bottom of each tomato to keep them from rolling. Spoon the filling into the shells. Garnish with parsley sprigs, if desired.

Makes 6 servings
Per serving: 240 calories, 6g protein, 34g carbohydrates, 10g fat, 1g saturated fat, 0mg cholesterol, 264mg sodium

---

Time Savers

GO WITH COUSCOUS FOR THE FASTEST FILLING

Couscous is the ideal side for the Quick Cook—one that's ready in minutes. Made from coarsely ground pale yellow semolina (that's the wheat flour traditionally used for pasta), the semolina is combined with water and salt to form a dough that is then rolled into tiny balls, which fluff up when boiling water is added.

Couscous is a mainstay in North African cookery, as well as in parts of Italy and areas throughout the Mediterranean. Israeli couscous is much larger than other forms. Either one is terrific as a salad or when used as stuffing for vegetables, as in our stuffed tomato recipe.

In the United States, couscous is easily found in large supermarkets or in Middle Eastern specialty markets.

Parmesan Garlic Bread, page 111

From the Bread Basket

Although the bread basket might arrive before anything else, it's definitely an important side to every meal. The next time you're serving roast beef, bake a batch of the popping-up popovers. When chicken's frying in the skillet or barbecuing on the grill, stir up some Sweet Potato Biscuits to serve alongside. And when you're planning pasta for supper, serve a loaf of Parmesan Garlic Bread—it'll be ready as fast as the pasta pot. Shape and bake Cheese Twists easily from frozen puff pastry. Try baking banana bread in small muffin rounds to save half the baking time. Plus, learn how to season store-bought breadsticks fast. You'll be serving delicious hot breads as quick as a flash.

WHAT KIND OF BISCUITS DO YOU MAKE?

❝I have a *very basic buttermilk biscuit recipe.* It calls for 2 cups of all-purpose flour, 2 teaspoons of baking powder, and ½ teaspoon of baking soda along with 1 teaspoon of salt. To that, I cut in 6 tablespoons of unsalted butter that I have cut into pieces, and then end by gently stirring in ⅔ to ¾ cup of buttermilk. I have fun altering the recipe!

Around the holidays, I like to add *1 tablespoon of grated orange zest and 2 teaspoons of dried sage* to the dough—perfect with the turkey.

Sometimes I make a *cinnamon-sugar mixture* that I sprinkle heavily over the biscuits just before I bake them. The aroma is amazing!

When I feel like a heartier biscuit, I toss about *1½ cups of shredded Cheddar cheese* into the flour mixture once the butter has been cut in. Sometimes I toss in about 2 to 3 tablespoons of chopped chives, too.

One of the easiest ways I vary the recipe is to add ¼ *cup of mixed chopped fresh herbs* to the butter-flour mixture. Fragrant and flavorful!❞

SuperQuick
SWEET POTATO BISCUITS

Prep **15 MINUTES**   *Bake* **10 MINUTES**

These slightly sweet and temptingly spice-scented biscuits will be a welcome addition to your next Thanksgiving dinner. Make them early in the day, then reheat them in a warm oven.

3	cups all-purpose flour
¾	cup packed brown sugar
1	tablespoon baking powder
1	teaspoon ground cinnamon
1	teaspoon ground ginger
1	teaspoon ground allspice
¾	teaspoon salt
½	cup butter, cut into pieces
1	cup cut-up canned yams, mashed
½	cup milk
½	cup chopped pecans

LET'S BEGIN Preheat the oven to 450°F. Grease a large cookie sheet.

MIX IT UP Combine the first 7 ingredients in a large bowl. Cut in the butter with a pastry cutter or two knives. Combine the yams and milk in a small bowl and stir into the flour mixture. Add the pecans. Knead the mixture in the bowl until combined. Transfer to a lightly floured surface and knead until smooth.

ROLL & BAKE Roll out the dough on a lightly floured surface to ½-inch thickness. Cut out biscuits with a 2-inch round cutter. Place 2 inches apart on the cookie sheet. Bake for 10 to 15 minutes, until lightly browned. Transfer to wire racks to cool.

Makes 10 servings
Per serving: 350 calories, 5g protein, 51g carbohydrates, 14g fat, 6g saturated fat, 27mg cholesterol, 338mg sodium

CHEDDAR ONION BISCUITS

Prep **15 MINUTES**   *Bake* **10 MINUTES**

1	tablespoon butter
1	large onion, chopped (1 cup)
2	cups all-purpose baking mix
⅔	cup milk
½	cup shredded mild Cheddar cheese

Drop biscuits are every bit as delicious as cut-out biscuits, and they take less time to make. Serve these, piled up in your favorite basket, along with a steaming pot of soup and a bowl of crisp salad greens for an absolutely perfect lunch or light supper.

LET'S BEGIN Preheat the oven to 425°F. Lightly grease a large baking sheet. Melt the butter in a small skillet over medium heat. Add the onion and cook, stirring occasionally, for 9 minutes, or until tender and golden brown.

MIX IT UP Transfer the onion to a medium bowl. Add all of the remaining ingredients. Mix just until the dry ingredients are moistened.

INTO THE OVEN Drop 12 heaping tablespoons of batter onto the baking sheet. Bake for 10 minutes, or until golden brown. Serve warm or at room temperature.

Makes 12 biscuits

Per biscuit: 133 calories, 5g protein, 22g carbohydrates, 3g fat, 2g saturated fat, 8mg cholesterol, 262mg sodium

PARMESAN BACON BISCUIT STICKS
Prep **15 MINUTES**   *Bake* **10 MINUTES**

1¼	cups all-purpose flour
¼	cup + 1 tablespoon grated Parmesan cheese
2	teaspoons baking powder
1	teaspoon Italian seasoning
⅛	teaspoon salt
¼	cup cold butter
⅔	cup + 1 tablespoon milk or half-and-half
2	tablespoons real bacon bits

The key to making these delicious biscuit sticks as light as possible is using a light hand when kneading and only long enough for the dough to become smooth. Keep in mind that the dough doesn't have to look "perfect."

LET'S BEGIN Preheat the oven to 425°F. Combine the flour, ¼ cup of the cheese, the baking powder, Italian seasoning, and salt in a large bowl. Cut in the butter with two knives used scissor-fashion until the mixture resembles coarse crumbs. Stir in ⅔ cup of the milk and the bacon bits. Mix just until the flour mixture is moistened.

SHAPE & ROLL On a lightly floured surface, knead the dough 5 to 8 times or until smooth. Roll out the dough to a 10 × 6-inch rectangle. Cut into 10 (1-inch) strips. Place 2 inches apart on a large ungreased cookie sheet. Brush the tops with the remaining 1 tablespoon milk and sprinkle with the remaining 1 tablespoon cheese.

INTO THE OVEN Bake for 10 to 12 minutes, until lightly browned. Transfer to wire racks. Serve warm or cool completely.

Makes 10 biscuit sticks

Per biscuit stick: 120 calories, 4g protein, 13g carbohydrates, 6g fat, 3g saturated fat, 15mg cholesterol, 220mg sodium

TENDER POPOVERS

Prep **10 MINUTES** *Bake* **35 MINUTES**

3	**large eggs, at room temperature**
1¼	**cups milk, at room temperature**
1¼	**cups all-purpose flour**
¼	**teaspoon salt**

Popovers are always a treat. They are made from a simple batter that has a high proportion of liquid. When heated in the oven, the liquid creates steam and the popovers puff up gloriously high. The name is derived from the fact that popovers seem to "pop" over the tops of the pans.

LET'S BEGIN Preheat the oven to 450°F. Grease six 5-ounce popover-pan cups or six 6-ounce custard cups with vegetable shortening. Heat the pan or cups in the oven for 5 minutes.

MIX IT UP Meanwhile, beat the eggs in a small bowl with an electric mixer on medium speed, scraping the bowl often, until light and lemon-colored. Add the milk and beat for 1 minute. Add the flour and salt and beat until well mixed.

INTO THE OVEN Pour the batter into the hot pan. Bake for 15 minutes. Reduce the oven temperature to 350°F. (Do not open the oven door.) Bake 20 to 25 minutes longer, until golden brown. Insert a small, sharp knife in the top of each popover to allow the steam to escape. Unmold and serve immediately.

Makes 6 popovers

Per popover: 160 calories, 8g protein, 23g carbohydrates, 4g fat, 2g saturated fat, 110mg cholesterol, 154mg sodium

PARMESAN GARLIC BREAD

Prep **10 MINUTES**   *Bake* **15 MINUTES**

1   **loaf (8 ounces) French bread, cut lengthwise in half**

2   **tablespoons butter or margarine, softened**

2   **garlic cloves, minced**

½   **cup part-skim mozzarella cheese**

¼   **cup grated Parmesan cheese**

The easiest way to peel garlic is to lightly press down on each clove with the side of a large knife until the skin pulls away. Then just remove the skin and trim off the hard end of each clove.

LET'S BEGIN Preheat the oven to 350°F. Place the bread cut side up in a large shallow baking pan.

MIX IT UP Combine the butter and garlic in a small bowl until well blended. Spread evenly onto the bread halves and sprinkle with the mozzarella and Parmesan.

BAKE & SERVE Bake for 15 minutes, or until the cheeses melt. Cut each bread half crosswise into 6 slices. Serve warm.

Makes 6 slices

Per slice: 190 calories, 8g protein, 22g carbohydrates, 8g fat, 3g saturated fat, 10mg cholesterol, 400mg sodium

Cooking Basics

MAKING PERFECT POPOVERS

If you've never discovered how quickly homemade popovers can impress your guests, you're in for a pleasant surprise. The best part is that they're fast and simple to make—and oh so delicious! Plus, you don't need a special popover pan to bake them. They bake just fine in a muffin pan or custard cups.

Here are some tips for mixing and baking perfect popovers:
• To begin, preheat the oven to 450°F and put the pan inside the oven for a few minutes to warm. Be sure the eggs and milk are at room temperature before starting (this lets the popovers start rising right away when you put them into the oven).
• Mix it right—Beat the batter until it's almost smooth, but don't worry if it has a few lumps.
• Into the oven—Bake the popovers for half the time in the hot preheated oven, then lower the temperature to 350°F.
• No peeking, please!—Never open the oven to sneak a peek at popovers while they're baking, as the cool air may cause the popovers to collapse.
• Out of the oven—The popovers are done when they're crispy brown on the outside and hollow and moist inside. Remove them from the pan immediately and pierce the side of each with a sharp knife (this lets the steam escape and keeps the outside crisp).
• Flavor 'em up!—Popovers are delicious as is, especially when served with a flavored butter such as strawberry or honey butter. For savory popovers, add some dried thyme or dill to the batter. For popovers to serve with roast beef, add grated Cheddar or crumbled blue cheese to the batter.

BREAD MACHINE GARLIC DINNER ROLLS

Prep 1½ HOURS + RISING   Bake 15 MINUTES

Using a bread machine makes it very easy to enjoy bakery-style bread or rolls just about any time you like, without a lot of work or fuss.

3	tablespoons butter or margarine, softened
1	cup warm water (105°F to 115°F)
⅓	cup instant nonfat dry milk
3	tablespoons sugar
1	teaspoon salt
1	teaspoon garlic powder
3	cups bread flour
1	package active dry yeast
1	large egg white
2	tablespoons water

LET'S BEGIN In the order listed above, place all the ingredients except the egg white in a bread machine pan. Set the machine on the Dough cycle and press Start.

SHAPE & LET RISE Lightly grease a large cookie sheet. When the cycle is finished, remove the dough from the machine. On a lightly floured surface, divide the dough into 12 equal pieces and shape each piece into a ball. Transfer the balls to the cookie sheet. Cover with a damp cloth and let rise in a warm, draft-free place for about 45 minutes, or until doubled in size.

INTO THE OVEN Preheat the oven to 350°F. Whisk the egg white and water together in a small bowl. Lightly brush over the tops of the rolls. Bake for 15 minutes, or until light golden brown. Serve warm.

Makes 12 rolls

Per roll: 173 calories, 5g protein, 29g carbohydrates, 4g fat, 2g saturated fat, 8mg cholesterol, 232mg sodium

Time Savers

5 FAST WAYS TO FLAVOR STORE-BOUGHT BREADSTICKS!

Here are some fast and easy ways to flavor store-bought plain breadsticks:

First, brush the breadsticks with a little water, then sprinkle on the seasonings. Try:

• Coarse sea salt and freshly ground black pepper
• Poppy seeds
• Sesame seeds
• Grated Parmesan cheese, plus a pinch of cayenne
• Onion or garlic salt and freshly ground black pepper
• Cajun seasoning

If you wish, you can put the flavored-up breadsticks on a baking sheet and warm them in a 350°F oven for about 5 minutes.

CHEESE TWISTS

Prep **15 MINUTES + THAWING**   *Bake* **10 MINUTES**

Cheese twists, especially easy homemade ones, make a great appetizer. Use just one type of cheese or a mix, if you prefer. Any combination will be fabulous.

½   **package (17¼ ounces) frozen puff pastry sheets (1 sheet)**

1   **large egg**

1   **tablespoon water**

2   **to 3 tablespoons grated Wisconsin Asiago, Parmesan, or Romano cheese**

Poppy seeds

LET'S BEGIN Thaw the puff pastry sheet at room temperature for 30 minutes. Preheat the oven to 400°F. Unfold the pastry onto a lightly floured surface. Roll out to a 14 × 10-inch rectangle. Cut lengthwise in half to make two 14 × 5-inch rectangles.

TWIST 'EM Beat the egg and water together in a small bowl. Brush each rectangle with the egg mixture. Sprinkle one rectangle with the cheese and the other with poppy seeds. Sandwich the rectangles with the egg-brushed sides together. Roll into a 14-inch square very gently so the rectangles stick together. Cut the pastry crosswise into twenty-eight ½-inch-thick strips. Lightly brush the strips with the egg mixture and sprinkle with poppy seeds. Twist the strips into corkscrew shapes and place on a large, ungreased cookie sheet.

INTO THE OVEN Bake for 10 to 12 minutes, until puffed and golden brown. Transfer the twists to wire racks and cool completely.

Makes 28 twists

Per twist: 60 calories, 1g protein, 4g carbohydrates, 4g fat, 1g saturated fat, 8mg cholesterol, 30mg sodium

ZESTY SPINACH BREAD

Prep **15 MINUTES**   *Bake* **12 MINUTES**

2 tablespoons olive oil

1 medium onion, finely chopped

2 garlic cloves, finely chopped

1 package (10 ounces) frozen chopped spinach, thawed and squeezed dry

2 teaspoons Worcestershire sauce

¼ teaspoon ground black pepper

1 (1 pound) Italian bread shell

1 medium tomato, seeded and chopped

2 cups shredded pizza double cheese blend

It is important to seed the tomato to remove all of the tomato's juice and prevent the bread from becoming soggy. If you have not seeded a tomato before, see page 33 for an easy how-to.

LET'S BEGIN Preheat the oven to 400°F. Heat the oil in a medium skillet over medium heat. Add the onion and garlic and sauté for 4 minutes, or until tender. Stir in the spinach, Worcestershire sauce, and pepper.

FIX IT FAST Spread the spinach mixture evenly over the bread shell. Top with the tomato and sprinkle evenly with the cheese.

INTO THE OVEN Bake for 12 minutes, or until heated through and the cheese melts. Cut into 8 wedges.

Makes 8 servings

Per serving: 297 calories, 13g protein, 34g carbohydrates, 12g fat, 5g saturated fat, 20mg cholesterol, 561mg sodium

Fiesta Cornbread

Prep **10 minutes** *Bake* **30 minutes**

2   cups all-purpose flour

1½ cups cornmeal

1½ cups shredded mild
    Cheddar cheese

1   can (7 ounces) diced
    green chiles

½   cup sugar

1   tablespoon baking
    powder

1½ teaspoons salt

1½ cups evaporated milk

½   cup vegetable oil

2   large eggs, lightly beaten

Lots of grated Cheddar cheese and green chiles make this cornbread recipe a favorite.

LET'S BEGIN Preheat the oven to 375°F. Grease a 13 × 9-inch baking dish. Mix the first 7 ingredients.

MIX IT UP Add the evaporated milk, oil, and eggs and stir just until the mixture is moistened. Spread into the dish.

INTO THE OVEN Bake for 30 to 35 minutes, until a wooden toothpick inserted in the center comes out clean. Cool in the pan on a wire rack for 10 minutes. Cut into twelve 3-inch squares. Serve warm.

Makes 12 squares

Per square: 365 calories, 10g protein, 41g carbohydrates, 17g fat, 6g saturated fat, 59mg cholesterol, 550mg sodium

ROASTED GARLIC TOAST

Prep **15 MINUTES**   *Cook* **4 MINUTES**

1	head garlic, papery skin removed
2	tablespoons dry white wine
2	tablespoons melted butter
8	slices French bread, toasted

Using the microwave is the quickest way to roast garlic. You can also use the roasted garlic to flavor mashed potatoes, a basic vinaigrette, and just about any steamed vegetable you like.

LET'S BEGIN Place the garlic in a glass measuring cup. Drizzle with the wine and melted butter.

COOK & SERVE Cover and microwave on High for 4 minutes, or until the garlic is soft. Cool, covered, for 5 minutes. Separate the garlic cloves and remove the garlic from the skins. To serve, mash the garlic onto one side of each slice of toast.

Makes 4 servings

Per serving: 210 calories, 5g protein, 29g carbohydrates, 8g fat, 3g saturated fat, 16mg cholesterol, 350mg sodium

---

Food Fact

CORNBREAD DOWN THROUGH THE CENTURIES

During the first year the colonists were in the New World, they learned ways to use corn from the Native Americans. They discovered that cornmeal was as valuable as flour in making their daily bread. They made simple ash cakes from cornmeal, which they baked right in the ashes of the fire, and hoecakes that they cooked on a hoe blade in front of the fire. One of the earliest breads made from corn was called corn pone, which was stirred from only three ingredients: cornmeal, water, and salt. As recipes were perfected, corn pone became known as

cornbread, and it was baked directly over the coals in a three-legged iron skillet called a spider.

Over the years, cornbread has become a tradition. It's baked into cornsticks in the Deep South in heavy cast-iron pans. The folks in Rhode Island use stone-ground white cornmeal to make corn cakes, which they bake on a griddle and call jonnycakes (no "h," please!), perhaps because they were compact and sturdy enough to travel (journey) well.

Along the battle lines between the North and the South during the Civil War, hush puppies were

created. Whenever Southern soldiers heard the enemy approaching, they would fry up bits of cornbread and throw them to the yelping dogs to quiet them, saying "Hush, puppy!" These small rounds of fried cornbread are still served throughout the South, especially along with fried fish.

But perhaps one of the most delicate creations from cornmeal are the famous spoonbreads, which bake up light and delicious—almost more like a custardy soufflé than a bread. Bet you can't stop with only one serving!

CLASSIC BANANA BREAD

Prep **20 MINUTES**   *Bake* **55 MINUTES**

Banana nut bread has become a favorite way to use up ripe bananas. Why not bake an extra loaf and freeze it?

2	cups all-purpose flour
1	teaspoon baking powder
½	teaspoon baking soda
½	teaspoon each salt and ground cinnamon
½	cup margarine, softened
¾	cup packed brown sugar
2	large eggs
2	ripe medium bananas, mashed (about 1 cup)
¼	cup sour cream
1	teaspoon vanilla extract
1	cup chopped almonds or walnuts, toasted

LET'S BEGIN Preheat the oven to 350°F. Spray a 9 × 5-inch loaf pan with cooking spray. Combine the flour, baking powder, baking soda, salt, and cinnamon in a medium bowl.

MIX IT UP Beat the margarine and brown sugar in a large bowl with an electric mixer on medium-high speed until light and fluffy. Beat in the eggs. Beat in the banana, sour cream, and vanilla until blended. Reduce the speed to low. Blend in the flour mixture. Stir in the almonds and pour into the pan.

INTO THE OVEN Bake for 55 to 65 minutes, until a wooden toothpick inserted in the center comes out clean. Cool in the pan on a wire rack for 10 minutes. Remove from the pan and cool completely on the rack.

Makes 12 slices

Per slice: 228 calories, 4g protein, 28g carbohydrates, 11g fat, 2g saturated fat, 15mg cholesterol, 206mg sodium

CRANBERRY ALMOND BREAD

Prep **15 MINUTES**   *Bake* **1 HOUR 15 MINUTES**

2   cups all-purpose flour

½   cup sugar +
     1 tablespoon, divided

2   teaspoons baking powder

1   teaspoon salt

1   large egg

½   cup butter, melted

¼   cup milk

2   teaspoons almond
     extract

1½   cups fresh or frozen
     cranberries

¼   cup sliced almonds

This recipe is a keeper! When fresh cranberries are in season during the fall and early winter, be sure to stock up so you can make this bread throughout the year. Simply put the packaged cranberries into the freezer and use them frozen.

LET'S BEGIN Preheat the oven to 375°F. Grease an 8½ × 4½-inch loaf pan. Combine the flour, ½ cup sugar, baking powder, and salt in a medium bowl.

MIX IT UP Combine the egg, melted butter, milk, and almond extract in another medium bowl. Add to the flour mixture and mix just until the flour mixture is moistened. Stir in the cranberries. Spread the batter in the pan. Sprinkle with remaining sugar and almonds.

INTO THE OVEN Bake for 45 minutes. Reduce the oven temperature to 350°F. Bake 30 minutes longer, or until a wooden toothpick inserted in the center comes out clean. Cool in the pan on a wire rack for 15 minutes. Remove the bread from the pan and cool completely on the rack.

Makes 12 slices

Per slice: 218 calories, 4g protein, 28g carbohydrates, 10g fat, 5g saturated fat, 40mg cholesterol, 366mg sodium

ASIAGO BREAD

Prep **40 MINUTES + RISING**   *Bake* **30 MINUTES**

1	package active dry yeast
¾	cup warm water (105°F to 115°F)
2	tablespoons sugar
3	cups all-purpose flour
1¾	teaspoons garlic salt
4	large eggs
½	cup butter or margarine, softened
1	cup shredded Asiago cheese
2	tablespoons dried basil

Asiago is a semi-firm Italian cheese that is made from cow's milk. It has a rich, nutty flavor. When it is aged for at least one year, it becomes hard enough to be considered good for shredding. It's especially fine in this bread. To speed up the rising time, let the dough rise on the upper rack of a cold oven with a bowl of hot water placed on the rack below.

LET'S BEGIN Combine the yeast and warm water in the large bowl of a heavy-duty mixer. Stir in the sugar, 1 cup of the flour, and 1¼ teaspoons of the garlic salt on low speed. Increase the speed to medium and beat well. Add 3 of the eggs, one at a time, beating well after each addition. Beat in the butter. Add the remaining 2 cups flour to make a soft dough.

SHAPE & LET RISE Grease a large bowl. On a lightly floured surface, knead the dough for 5 minutes, or until smooth and elastic. Place the dough in the bowl. Cover with a clean kitchen towel and let rise in a warm, draft-free place for about 40 minutes, or until doubled in size. Grease two 9 × 5-inch bread pans. Combine the cheese, basil, the remaining egg, and the remaining ½ teaspoon garlic salt in a small bowl. Knead the dough lightly. Roll out into a 10 × 16-inch rectangle. Spread the cheese mixture over the dough and roll up lengthwise. Cut the roll in half and place each piece in a pan. Cover and let rise until doubled in size.

INTO THE OVEN Preheat the oven to 350°F. Bake the loaves 30 to 35 minutes, or until the tops are browned and each loaf sounds hollow when tapped on the bottom. Cool the loaves in the pans for 15 minutes. Unmold and cool completely on wire racks. Cut each loaf into 10 slices.

Makes 20 slices
Per slice: 146 calories, 5g protein, 15g carbohydrates, 7g fat, 5g saturated fat, 59mg cholesterol, 273mg sodium

On the Menu

In Ireland, St. Patrick's Day is celebrated by wearing green clothing and eating green food. Join in the celebration!

Cups of Puréed Green Pea Soup

Dollops of Sour Cream

Traditional Corned Beef and Cabbage

Mustard Sauce

Parsleyed-Butter Potatoes

Warm Irish Soda Bread

Irish Coffee

Sweetened Whipped Cream

Frosted Cupcakes Topped with Green Sprinkles

IRISH SODA BREAD

Prep **15 MINUTES**   Bake **1 HOUR**

Irish soda bread is a type of quick bread—meaning a bread that is leavened with baking powder or baking soda instead of yeast. It is quick to prepare and very tasty. For a true breakfast or teatime treat, slice, toast, and lightly spread the bread with butter.

3¼   cups all-purpose flour

⅓   cup + 1 tablespoon sugar

1   teaspoon baking powder

1   teaspoon baking soda

1   teaspoon salt

½   cup cold butter

1⅓   cups buttermilk

½   cup currants or raisins

LET'S BEGIN Preheat the oven to 350°F. Grease a large baking sheet.

MIX IT UP Combine the flour, ⅓ cup of the sugar, the baking powder, baking soda, and salt in a large bowl. Cut in the butter with a pastry cutter until the mixture resembles coarse crumbs. Add the buttermilk and currants and mix just until moistened.

SHAPE & BAKE On a floured surface, knead the dough 10 times. Shape into a 2½-inch-thick round loaf. Place on the baking sheet. With a small, sharp knife, cut a ½-inch-deep "X" in the top of the loaf. Sprinkle with the remaining 1 tablespoon sugar. Bake for 1 hour, or until golden brown. Cool completely on a wire rack. Cut into 16 wedges.

Makes 16 servings

Per serving: 170 calories, 3g protein, 26g carbohydrates, 6g fat, 4g saturated fat, 15mg cholesterol, 340mg sodium

Sweet Potato Pies, page 138

Sweets on the Side

Who said you have to wait for dessert to have a little something sweet? Here are side dishes that work swell as part of the main meal, but at the same time they help satisfy your sweet tooth, before dessert arrives. In fact, with these sides served at dinner, you can skip dessert altogether! Serve a small flan alongside slices of roast chicken, ladle up some sautéed apples and onions the next time you grill pork chops, or bake a fresh pear gratin for a winter's feast. Bring on the bread pudding any time you wish, and stir some rice pudding in just 15 minutes. Then check out the many different ways to stuff those forever-favorite baked apples. You and your family will be glad you did!

CARAMELIZED ORANGE FLAN

Prep **20 MINUTES**   *Bake* **45 MINUTES + CHILLING**

2¼ cups freshly squeezed
orange juice

6   large egg yolks

3   large eggs

1½ cups sugar

Pinch of salt

3   cups heavy cream

1   (3-inch) cinnamon stick

¼   cup water

This is great for making a day ahead. Then all you have to do is unmold the custards onto serving plates.

LET'S BEGIN Preheat the oven to 300°F. Bring the orange juice to a boil in a small heavy saucepan. Reduce the heat to medium and cook until reduced to 1 cup. In a medium bowl, whisk the egg yolks, eggs, ¾ cup of the sugar, and salt together. Whisk in the reduced orange juice. Combine the cream and cinnamon stick in a small saucepan. Cook, stirring, over medium-high heat until small bubbles appear around the edge of the pan. Remove from the heat, remove the cinnamon stick, and whisk the cream into the orange juice mixture.

COOK IT To make the caramel, cook the remaining ¾ cup sugar and the water in a clean small heavy saucepan. Cook over medium heat until the sugar dissolves. Increase the heat to high and cook until it turns a golden amber. Quickly pour into 8 individual ramekins. Set aside until the caramel hardens.

BAKE & CHILL Fill the ramekins with the orange custard. Place the ramekins in a large baking pan. Place in the center of the oven and add enough hot water to the baking pan to come halfway up the sides of the ramekins. Cover with foil. Bake for 45 to 50 minutes, until the flans are just set. Carefully remove the ramekins from the water. Refrigerate at least 5 hours or overnight. To unmold, run the tip of a small knife around the inside edge of each ramekin and invert onto a plate.

Makes 8 servings
Per serving: 550 calories, 7g protein, 46g carbohydrates, 39g fat, 23g saturated fat, 356mg cholesterol, 104mg sodium

WISCONSIN BRIE AND FRUIT PIE

Prep **20 MINUTES**   *Bake* **30 MINUTES + STANDING**

1   wheel (14 ounces)
    Wisconsin Brie cheese

1   (9-inch) unbaked
    piecrust

1   can (21 ounces) fruit
    pie filling (apple, cherry,
    peach, or blueberry)

Fruit and cheese is a match made in heaven. Here they come together in a pie to create a special treat that is sure to impress.

LET'S BEGIN Preheat the oven to 400°F. Place the cheese in the center of the piecrust. Spoon the pie filling over the top and around the cheese.

BAKE & LET STAND Bake for 30 to 35 minutes, until the cheese softens and the fruit filling is bubbly. Let stand at room temperature for at least 1 hour, or until set. Serve warm.

Makes 8 servings

Per serving: 363 calories, 12g protein, 31g carbohydrates, 21g fat, 10g saturated fat, 49mg cholesterol, 438mg sodium

RAISIN & ALMOND RISOTTO

Prep **15 MINUTES**   *Cook* **25 MINUTES**

¼   cup unsalted butter

2   cups Arborio rice

½   cup golden raisins +
    extra for garnish
    (optional)

3   to 5 cups hot water

1½ cups hot milk

½   cup sugar

½   cup almonds, coarsely
    chopped and toasted

    Ground cinnamon

Arborio rice, a short-grain white rice, is appreciated for its ability to absorb liquid and to become creamy.

LET'S BEGIN Melt the butter in a large saucepan over medium heat. Stir in the rice and the ½ cup raisins until coated with the butter.

SIMMER & STIR Add the hot water, ½ cup at a time, stirring constantly, until the rice has absorbed the liquid after each addition. (When all the water has been added, the rice will still be crunchy, but should also begin to soften.) Add the hot milk, ½ cup at a time, stirring constantly after each addition, until the rice is creamy and al dente. Stir in the sugar.

SERVE Spoon the risotto on a serving plate. Garnish with the almonds and additional raisins, if you like. Sprinkle the top with cinnamon.

Makes 6 servings

Per serving: 488 calories, 9g protein, 83g carbohydrates, 16g fat, 7g saturated fat, 28mg cholesterol, 31mg sodium

GOLDEN PEAR GRATIN

Prep **30 MINUTES**   *Bake* **25 MINUTES**

½	cup honey
¼	cup dry white wine
1	tablespoon lemon juice
1	tablespoon orange juice
½	cup sliced almonds, toasted
1	tablespoon grated lemon zest
1	tablespoon grated orange zest
½	teaspoon ground cinnamon
2	pounds ripe pears, peeled, cored, and sliced

A gratin dish is a shallow baking dish that is heat-safe, so it can be put under the broiler or into the oven. But you can use any shallow baking dish or pie plate that you like.

LET'S BEGIN Preheat the oven to 400°F. Grease a 10-inch gratin dish or pie plate. Combine the honey, wine, lemon juice, and orange juice in a small saucepan. Bring to a boil, whisking to dissolve the honey. Reduce the heat and simmer for about 15 minutes, or until the liquid is reduced by half.

LAYER IT EASY Chop ¼ cup of the almonds. Transfer to a small bowl. Stir in the lemon zest, orange zest, and cinnamon until well mixed. Layer half the pear slices in the gratin dish. Sprinkle with the chopped almond mixture. Top with the remaining pear slices and the remaining ¼ cup sliced almonds. Pour the honey mixture over the pears.

INTO THE OVEN Bake for 25 minutes, or until the top is golden brown. Serve warm or cold.

Makes 6 servings
Per serving: 256 calories, 3g protein, 50g carbohydrates, 6g fat, 0g saturated fat, 0mg cholesterol, 3mg sodium

HONEY BAKED APPLES
Prep **5 MINUTES**   *Bake* **25 MINUTES**

3	apples, peeled and cored
1	teaspoon lemon juice
½	cup honey
¾	cup fresh or frozen cranberries
¼	cup chopped walnuts
¼	cup plain dry bread crumbs
1	tablespoon butter or margarine, melted
1	teaspoon ground cinnamon

Dash salt

Dash ground ginger

Dash ground nutmeg

Serve these honeylicious apples with ice cream for dessert or with sausage links for breakfast or brunch.

LET'S BEGIN Preheat the oven to 400°F. Lightly coat a small baking dish with vegetable oil. Cut 2 of the apples lengthwise in half and brush with the lemon juice. Place cut side down in the dish and brush with the honey. Cover the dish with foil and bake for 15 minutes.

MAKE TOPPING Meanwhile, chop the last apple and transfer to a medium bowl. Add the remaining ingredients and toss to mix well.

BAKE & BROWN Remove the apples from the oven and turn cut side up. Mound the topping on the apples. Bake, uncovered, 10 minutes longer, or until the topping browns. Serve warm.

Makes 4 servings

Per serving (½ apple each): 415 calories, 11g protein, 79g carbohydrates, 9g fat, 2g saturated fat, 8mg cholesterol, 93mg sodium

Cook to Cook

WHAT'S THE BEST WAY TO STUFF BAKED APPLES?

❝I like to save time by *cutting each apple through the stem end into two halves, which cuts the baking time in half.* I place the apple halves, without filling them yet, cut side down in a baking dish, and drizzle them with some honey or apple cider. After baking the apples for about half the regular time in a covered dish, I turn them over, fill them, then return the apples to the oven for the rest of the baking time.

In place of honey for the sweetening, *I often use maple syrup—plus a little orange zest* for added flavor. These apples are the perfect side dish for baked ham.

Another time, I'll fill the apples with *shredded Cheddar cheese and chives.* These are great to serve on the side with roast beef.

And around Valentine's Day, *I stuff apples with plenty of those tiny cinnamon hot candies and chopped pecans.* They melt in the oven, giving the apples a beautiful red glaze.❞

Fruit Salad with Honey-Orange Dressing
Prep **20 MINUTES**

½	cup plain low-fat yogurt
¼	cup nonfat mayonnaise
¼	cup honey
¾	teaspoon grated orange zest
¼	teaspoon dry mustard
3	tablespoons orange juice
1½	teaspoons vinegar
4	cups assorted fresh fruit

Here's a tasty fruit salad with a delectable dressing that is easy on the waistline! You can also use the dressing to spoon over cold chicken or salmon.

LET'S BEGIN Whisk the first 5 ingredients together in a small bowl until blended. Gradually whisk in the orange juice and vinegar.

TOSS & SERVE Toss the fruit gently with the dressing in a large bowl. Cover and refrigerate until ready to serve.

Makes 4 servings

Per serving: 168 calories, 3g protein, 41g carbohydrates, 1g fat, 0g saturated fat, 2mg cholesterol, 220mg sodium

Winter Fruit Compote
Prep **10 MINUTES + CHILLING**   *Cook* **15 MINUTES**

1	cup apple juice
¼	cup packed light brown sugar
¼	cup water
1	tablespoon lemon juice
½	cup dried apricot halves, quartered
½	cup dried whole figs, sliced
½	cup dried cranberries
1	teaspoon vanilla extract
½	teaspoon ground ginger
¼	teaspoon ground cinnamon

This compote will keep for up to 3 days in the refrigerator. Serve it for breakfast spooned over some plain yogurt and sprinkled with granola or over fat wedges of pound cake or angel food cake. A little whipped cream on the side isn't a bad idea either.

LET'S BEGIN Combine the apple juice, brown sugar, water, and lemon juice in a small saucepan. Bring to a simmer and cook, stirring, until the sugar dissolves.

SIMMER LOW Add the remaining ingredients. Simmer about 5 minutes longer, or until the fruit is plump and the liquid is slightly thickened.

LET IT CHILL Transfer the compote to a bowl. Cover and refrigerate until chilled.

Makes 4 servings

Per serving: 240 calories, 1g protein, 60g carbohydrates, 0g fat, 0g saturated fat, 0mg cholesterol, 12mg sodium

SCALLOPED APPLES & ONIONS

Prep **15 MINUTES**   *Bake* **25 MINUTES**

4   tablespoons butter, melted

1   medium onion, thinly sliced

5   red or green apples, cored and thinly sliced

1½   cups pasteurized processed cheese, cut into small pieces (8 ounces)

2   cups prepared french-fried onions

The easiest way to thinly slice apples is with a serrated bread knife. In fact, a serrated knife makes quick work of slicing lots of foods besides bread.

LET'S BEGIN Preheat the oven to 375°F. Grease a 9-inch deep-dish pie plate.

INTO THE SKILLET Heat 2 tablespoons of the butter in a medium skillet over medium-high heat. Sauté the onion for 3 minutes, or until tender. Add the apples and cook, stirring, for 5 minutes, or until the apples are tender. Stir in 1 cup of the cheese, 1 cup of the french-fried onions, and the remaining 2 tablespoons butter. Transfer to the pie plate.

INTO THE OVEN Bake for 20 minutes, or until hot. Add the remaining ½ cup cheese and 1 cup french-fried onions. Bake 5 minutes longer, or until the cheese melts.

Makes 6 servings

Per serving: 387 calories, 8g protein, 29g carbohydrates, 27g fat, 13g saturated fat, 46mg cholesterol, 823mg sodium

WHITE CHOCOLATE BREAD PUDDING

Prep **20 MINUTES**   *Bake* **40 MINUTES**

5   cups white bread cubes
     (sliced ½ inch thick)

1   package (6 ounces)
     white baking chocolate

2   cups half-and-half or
     milk

½   cup sugar

¼   cup butter or margarine

3   large eggs, lightly beaten

2   teaspoons vanilla extract

Chocolate Sauce (see recipe)

Bread pudding is the perfect way to use up leftover or slightly stale bread. Use plain white bread in bread pudding, or try brioche, challah, or even raisin bread.

LET'S BEGIN Preheat the oven to 325°F. Place the bread cubes in a 2-quart baking dish.

MIX IT UP Combine the chocolate, half-and-half, sugar, and butter in a large microwaveable bowl. Microwave on High for 4 minutes, stirring once and watching closely. When finished heating, stir until the chocolate is completely melted. Beat in the eggs and vanilla. Pour over the bread in the baking dish.

INTO THE OVEN Place the baking dish in a large baking pan. Place in the center of the oven and carefully add enough boiling water to come 1 inch up the sides of the baking dish. Bake for 40 to 45 minutes, until a knife inserted near the center of the pudding comes out almost clean. Serve warm with the chocolate sauce.

Time Savers

4 INCREDIBLE QUICK SAUCES FOR BREAD PUDDING

There are lots of quick ways to sauce up bread pudding without a lot of effort.
• Set out some high-quality vanilla ice cream until it melts—perfect sauce!
• Press a jar of apricot preserves through a sieve. Add a tablespoon or two of orange or apricot liqueur or orange juice—enough just to thin it!

• You can also stir heavy cream or half-and-half into fudge sauce until spoonable—fabulous!
• Thaw a bag of frozen raspberries, then puree them, adding a splash of crème de cassis black currant liqueur, if you like. Press through a sieve, ladle it over the bread pudding, and top it all off with a dollop of sour cream.

CHOCOLATE SAUCE

Combine 1 package (8 ounces) semisweet baking chocolate and 1 cup heavy cream in a large microwaveable bowl. Microwave on High for 4 minutes, or until the cream is simmering, stirring after 2 minutes. Whisk until the chocolate completely melts and the mixture is well blended.

Makes 8 servings
Per serving: 634 calories, 10g protein, 55g carbohydrates, 43g fat, 25g saturated fat, 163mg cholesterol, 277mg sodium

OLD-FASHIONED BREAD PUDDING WITH VANILLA SAUCE

Prep **10 MINUTES**   Bake **44 MINUTES + STANDING**

8	slices white bread, cubed (4 cups)
½	cup raisins
2	cups milk
¼	cup butter
½	cup sugar
2	large eggs, lightly beaten
1	teaspoon vanilla extract
½	teaspoon ground nutmeg

Vanilla Sauce (see recipe)

Letting the bread and milk mixture rest for 10 minutes guarantees that the bread will soak up enough of the liquid, making for a better bread pudding. The very easy and tempting vanilla-flavored sauce makes this pudding extra-special.

LET'S BEGIN Preheat the oven to 350°F. Grease a 1½-quart baking dish. Combine the bread cubes and raisins in a large bowl. Combine the milk and butter in a small saucepan. Cook over medium heat for 4 to 7 minutes, or until the butter melts. Pour the milk mixture over the bread mixture and let stand for 10 minutes.

INTO THE OVEN Stir the sugar, eggs, vanilla, and nutmeg into the bread mixture. Pour it into the baking dish. Bake for 40 to 50 minutes, or until set in the center.

MAKE IT SAUCY Meanwhile, make the Vanilla Sauce and ladle over the warm pudding right before serving.

VANILLA SAUCE

Combine in a small saucepan: ½ cup butter, ½ cup granulated sugar, ½ cup packed brown sugar, and ½ cup heavy cream. Cook, stirring occasionally, over medium heat for 5 to 8 minutes, until the mixture thickens and comes to a full boil. Stir in 1 teaspoon vanilla extract.

Makes 8 servings

Per serving: 470 calories, 6g protein, 56g carbohydrates, 26g fat, 13g saturated fat, 125mg cholesterol, 310mg sodium

CINNAMON RICE PUDDING

Prep **25 MINUTES**   *Cook* **20 MINUTES**

Cooking rice pudding is the perfect rainy day activity. And you end up with a fabulous dessert. Go ahead and splurge—serve it with whipped cream.

3	cups cooked medium-grain white rice
3	cups milk
½	cup sugar
¼	cup butter
2	(3-inch) cinnamon sticks
1	teaspoon vanilla extract

Ground cinnamon (optional)

Whipped cream (optional)

LET'S BEGIN Combine the cooked rice, milk, sugar, butter, and cinnamon sticks in a large saucepan. Cook over medium heat, stirring frequently, for 20 to 25 minutes, until thick and creamy.

SERVE Remove the pan from the heat. Remove the cinnamon sticks and stir in the vanilla. Sprinkle the top with ground cinnamon and serve with whipped cream, if you like.

Makes 6 servings

Per serving: 331 calories, 6g protein, 48g carbohydrates, 12g fat, 6g saturated fat, 38mg cholesterol, 143mg sodium

Cook to Cook

HOW DO YOU MAKE RICE PUDDING EXTRA SPECIAL?

❝ *I love rice pudding* and serve it almost every chance I get. So my friends and family don't get bored, I like to give it a new personality.

When berry season rolls around, I like to *spoon the rice pudding into parfait glasses, alternating with tempting layers of sweetened fresh mixed berries.* I then top off each rice pudding parfait with a generous dollop of whipped cream and a perfect berry.

For a perfect ending to a special dinner party, I put *tart cherry pie filling* into a sieve to remove most of the saucy part. I then put a layer of the cherry mixture in the bottom of ramekins, custard cups, or wine glasses, spoon in the rice pudding, and top it off with *toasted sliced almonds*— a delicious surprise for all.

I also think rice pudding is ideal for breakfast. I spoon servings into soup bowls and *sprinkle granola on top.* ❞

15-MINUTE AUTUMN RICE PUDDING
Prep **10 MINUTES** *Cook* **5 MINUTES**

3	cups milk
1	cup instant white rice
1	red or green apple, cored and chopped
⅓	cup dark raisins
½	teaspoon ground cinnamon
¼	teaspoon ground nutmeg
1	package (4-serving size) vanilla instant pudding and pie filling mix
¼	cup chopped walnuts (optional)

What could be better than preparing creamy rice pudding in under 20 minutes? Chopped apples add a pleasant crunch and good flavor, while the addition of warm spices makes it cozy and comforting. To save time, don't peel the apple.

LET'S BEGIN Bring 1 cup of the milk to a boil in a medium saucepan. Stir in the rice, apple, raisins, cinnamon, and nutmeg. Cover and remove from the heat. Let stand 5 minutes.

STIR Meanwhile, prepare the pudding mix with the remaining 2 cups milk in a large bowl according to package directions.

MIX & SERVE Add the rice mixture to the pudding and mix well. Stir in the walnuts, if you like. Cover with plastic and cool for 5 minutes. Serve warm or chilled.

Makes 8 servings
Per serving: 160 calories, 4g protein, 32g carbohydrates, 2g fat, 1g saturated fat, 5mg cholesterol, 220mg sodium

ALMOND TUILE COOKIE CUPS

Prep **20 MINUTES**   *Bake* **3 MINUTES + COOKING**

Tuile, French for "tile," is a thin, crisp cookie that is usually draped over a custard cup or rolling pin while hot to give it a special shape. Here they are shaped into delicate cups that are ideal for filling with scoops of luscious fruit sorbet or ice cream—or both!

¼	cup butter, softened
⅓	cup packed light brown sugar
¼	teaspoon grated orange zest
¼	teaspoon almond extract
2	large egg whites
⅓	cup all-purpose flour
⅓	cup sliced natural almonds, toasted

LET'S BEGIN Preheat the oven to 400°F. Generously coat 2 large cookie sheets with cooking spray.

MIX & SPREAD Cream the butter and brown sugar in a medium bowl with an electric mixer on medium speed until light and fluffy. Beat in the orange zest and almond extract. Beat in the egg whites just until blended. Stir in the flour and almonds just until blended. Drop 2 rounded tablespoonfuls of the dough 4 inches apart on each cookie sheet. Spread the dough into 6-inch circles with the back of a spoon.

BAKE & SHAPE Bake for 3 to 4 minutes, or until the edges are golden brown but the centers are light in color. Immediately drape the hot cookies over custard cups, pressing in the sides to form cup shapes. Cool the cookies completely, then remove from the cups.

Makes 6 cookies

Per cookie: 180 calories, 3g protein, 18g carbohydrates, 11g fat, 4g saturated fat, 22mg cholesterol, 81mg sodium

---

Cook to Cook

TUILES LOOK SO FANCY—ARE THEY REALLY HARD TO MAKE?

❝Not at all! *These curled wafer cookies* are often presented at the end of a special meal along with coffee and chocolate truffles. They can also be used to hold a side serving of a vegetable or salad alongside the entrée, such as the Orange & Beet Salad (page 32).

They get their curved shape *by being draped while still rather hot over a rolling pin or custard cup until they are set and firm.*

The trick is to quickly move the hot cookies from the cookie sheet before they cool and harden. The easiest way to accomplish this is to *use a wide spatula that has a thin blade.*

If the cookies cool before you have a chance to shape them, *return them to the oven for a couple of minutes to warm and soften.* Once the shaped cookies are firm, transfer them to wire racks to cool. ❞

SWEET POTATO PIES

Prep **20 MINUTES**   *Cook* **1 ½ HOURS**

2   large or 3 medium sweet potatoes

½   cup butter or margarine, softened

1   cup granulated sugar

⅔   cup evaporated milk

2   large eggs, beaten

2   tablespoons packed brown sugar

1   teaspoon vanilla extract

1   teaspoon lemon juice

1   teaspoon ground cinnamon

¼   teaspoon ground nutmeg

⅛   teaspoon salt

2   (9-inch) unbaked piecrusts

Whipped cream

Sweet potato pie, a great Southern tradition, is a nice change from pies such as pumpkin or pecan. If you can find medium sweet potatoes in your market, choose them as they will take less time to cook.

LET'S BEGIN Combine the potatoes and enough water to cover in a large saucepan. Bring to a boil. Reduce the heat and cook for 45 to 50 minutes, until tender. Drain. Cool slightly and peel.

MAKE FILLING Preheat the oven to 425°F. Transfer the warm potatoes to a large bowl. Add the butter and mash the potatoes. Stir in the granulated sugar, evaporated milk, eggs, brown sugar, vanilla, lemon juice, cinnamon, nutmeg, and salt until blended. Pour into the 2 crusts, dividing the filling evenly.

INTO THE OVEN Bake for 15 minutes. Reduce the oven temperature to 350°F. Bake 30 to 40 minutes longer, until a knife inserted near the center of each pie comes out clean. Cool the pies on wire racks for 2 hours. Top with whipped cream. Serve immediately or refrigerate.

Makes 16 servings

Per serving: 290 calories, 3g protein, 30g carbohydrates, 18g fat, 7g saturated fat, 56mg cholesterol, 205mg sodium

CREDITS

PAGE 2 McCormick: Photo for Black Beans 'n' Rice courtesy of McCormick. Used with permission.

PAGE 8 Sargento: Photo for Cheddar-Stuffed Spuds courtesy of Sargento Foods Inc. Used with permission.

PAGE 12 Kraft Foods: Photo for Irish Soda Bread courtesy of Kraft Kitchens. Used with permission.

PAGE 17 Cherry Marketing Institute: Photo for Squash Bake courtesy of The Cherry Marketing Institute. Used with permission.

PAGE 18 Florida Tomato Committee: Photo for Green Beans & Fresh Tomato Sauce courtesy of the Florida Tomato Committee. Used with permission.

PAGE 20 CanolaInfo: Recipe for Mixed Greens with Maple Dressing courtesy of CanolaInfo. Used with permission.

PAGE 21 Sunkist: Recipe for Garden Fresh Coleslaw courtesy of Sunkist Growers, Inc. Used with permission.

PAGES 22/23 Dole: Photo and recipe for South of the Border Slaw courtesy of Dole Food Company. Used with permission.

PAGE 24 Wish-Bone: Recipe for Shrimp & Bean Salad courtesy of Wish-Bone®. Used with permission.

PAGE 25 Dole: Recipe and photo for Pineapple Black Bean Salad courtesy of Dole Food Company. Used with permission.

PAGE 26 CanolaInfo: Recipe for Black Bean & Corn Salad courtesy of CanolaInfo. Used with permission.

PAGE 27 Sunkist: Recipe for Easy Three-Bean Salad courtesy of Sunkist Growers, Inc. Used with permission.

PAGES 28/29 Land O'Lakes: Photo and recipe for Fresh Beans & Tomatoes with Dill Cream courtesy of Land O'Lakes, Inc. Used with permission.

PAGE 30 Wish-Bone: Recipe for Green Beans & Feta courtesy of Wish-Bone®. Used with permission.

PAGE 31 Earthbound Farm: Recipe for Broccoli Salad courtesy of Earthbound Farm. Used with permission.

PAGE 31 Bird's Eye: Recipe for Sunny Carrot Salad courtesy of Birds Eye Foods. Used with permission.

PAGE 32 French's: Recipe for Orange & Beet Salad courtesy of French's® mustard. Used with permission.

PAGE 33 Wish-Bone: Recipe for Mediterranean Tomato Salad courtesy of Wish-Bone®. Used with permission.

PAGE 34 Michigan Asparagus Advisory Board: Photo and recipe for Roasted Potatoes & Asparagus courtesy of the Michigan Asparagus Advisory Board. Used with permission.

PAGE 35 California Strawberry Commission: Recipe for Spinach & Asparagus Salad courtesy of the California Strawberry Commission®. Used with permission.

PAGE 36 Nestlé: Photo and recipe for Salad Italiano courtesy of Nestlé. Used with permission.

PAGE 37 CanolaInfo: Recipe for Tabbouleh Salad courtesy of CanolaInfo. Used with permission.

PAGE 38 Kraft Foods: Photo for Spring Risotto courtesy of Kraft Kitchens. Used with permission.

PAGE 40 Florida Tomato Committee: Recipe for Polenta with Tomato Salsa courtesy of the Florida Tomato Committee. Used with permission.

PAGE 41 Dole: Photo and recipe for Pineapple Wild Rice courtesy of Dole Food Company. Used with permission.

PAGE 42 American Egg Board: Recipe for Cinnamon-Noodle Kugel courtesy of the American Egg Board. Used with permission.

PAGE 43 McCormick: Photo and recipe for Savory Orzo courtesy of McCormick. Used with permission.

PAGES 44/45 United States Potato Board: Photo and recipe for Garlic Mashed Potatoes courtesy of the United States Potato Board. Used with permission.

PAGE 46 National Honey Board: Recipe for Honey-Mustard Roasted Potatoes courtesy of the National Honey Board. Used with permission.

PAGE 47 French's: Recipe for Easy Twice-Baked Potatoes courtesy of French's® French Fried Onions. Used with permission.

PAGE 48 Sargento: Recipe for Best Ever Potatoes Au Gratin courtesy of Sargento Foods Inc. Used with permission.

PAGE 49 Sargento: Photo and recipe for Cheesy Hash Brown Casserole courtesy of Sargento Foods Inc. Used with permission.

PAGES 50/51 United States Potato Board: Photo and recipe for Fun Fries courtesy of the United States Potato Board. Used with permission.

PAGE 52 United States Potato Board: Recipe for Touchdown 'Taters courtesy of the United States Potato Board. Used with permission.

PAGE 53 Bruce Foods: Recipe for Sweet Potato Soufflé courtesy of Bruce Foods Corporation. Used with permission.

PAGE 54 McCormick: Recipe for Candied Sweet Potatoes courtesy of McCormick. Used with permission.

PAGE 55 Kraft Foods: Photo and recipe for Double-Baked Sweet Potato courtesy of Kraft Kitchens. Used with permission.

PAGES 56/57 Kraft Foods: Photo and recipe for Spring Risotto courtesy of Kraft Kitchens. Used with permission.

PAGE 58 Ocean Spray Cranberries: Recipe for Fruited Rice Pilaf courtesy of Ocean Spray Cranberries, Inc. Used with permission.

PAGE 59 McCormick: Photo and recipe for Vegetable Fried Rice courtesy of McCormick. Used with permission.

PAGE 60 Uncle Ben's: Recipe for Harvest Rice courtesy of UNCLE BEN'S® Brand. Used with permission.

PAGES 60/61 McCormick: Photo and recipe for Black Beans 'n' Rice courtesy of McCormick. Used with permission.

PAGE 62 French's: Recipe for BBQ Baked Beans courtesy of French's French's® mustard and Cattlemen's® Barbecue Sauce. Used with permission.

PAGE 63 McCormick: Photo and recipe for Old-Fashioned Bean Bake courtesy of McCormick. Used with permission.

PAGE 64 Cherry Marketing Institute: Photo for Carrots with Character courtesy of The Cherry Marketing Institute. Used with permission.

PAGE 66 Almond Board of California: Recipe for Roasted Asparagus & Tomatoes with Almonds courtesy of the Almond Board of California. Used with permission.

PAGE 67 McCormick: Recipe for Vanilla Beans Amandine courtesy of McCormick. Used with permission.

PAGE 67 National Honey Board: Recipe for Honey-Glazed Carrots courtesy of the National Honey Board. Used with permission.

PAGE 68 Florida Tomato Committee: Photo and recipe for Green Beans & Fresh Tomato Sauce courtesy of the Florida Tomato Committee. Used with permission.

PAGE 69 McCormick: Recipe for Italian Vegetable Ragout courtesy of McCormick. Used with permission.

PAGE 70 Earthbound Farm: Recipe for Lemon-Rosemary Broccoli courtesy of Earthbound Farm. Used with permission.

PAGES 70/71 Cherry Marketing Institute: Photo and recipe for Carrots with Character courtesy of The Cherry Marketing Institute. Used with permission.

PAGE 72 Bird's Eye: Recipe for Brussels Sprouts wit Lemon Thyme courtesy of Bird's Eye Foods. Used with permission.

PAGE 73 Kraft Foods: Photo and recipe for Cheesy Cauliflower Bake courtesy of Kraft Kitchens. Used with permission.

PAGE 74 Produce for Better Health Foundation: Photo and recipe for Broccoli Red Pepper Stir-Fry courtesy of Produce for Better Health Foundation. Used with permission.

PAGE 75 Land O'Lakes: Recipe for Corn on the Cobb with Seasoned Butters courtesy of Land O'Lakes, Inc. Used with permission.

PAGE 76 Kraft Foods: Recipe for Southern Collard Greens courtesy of Kraft Kitchens. Used with permission.

PAGE 77 National Honey Board: Photo and recipe for Sweet & Hot Marinated Mushrooms courtesy of the National Honey Board. Used with permission.

PAGES 78/79 Cherry Marketing Institute: Photo and recipe for Squash Bake courtesy of The Cherry Marketing Institute. Used with permission.

PAGE 80 Sunkist: Recipe for Acorn Squash courtesy of Sunkist Growers, Inc. Used with permission.

PAGE 81 National Honey Board: Recipe for Peas with Pizzazz courtesy of the National Honey Board. Used with permission.

PAGE 81 McCormick: Recipe for Speedy Creamed Spinach courtesy of McCormick. Used with permission.

PAGE 82 National Honey Board: Photo and recipe for Sweet & Sour Zucchini courtesy of the National Honey Board. Used with permission.

PAGE 83 Florida Tomato Committee: Photo and recipe for Greek-Style Vegetables courtesy of the Florida Tomato Committee. Used with permission.

PAGE 84 Florida Tomato Committee: Photo for Tomatoes Stuffed with Couscous courtesy of the Florida Tomato Committee. Used with permission.

PAGES 86/87 Nestlé: Recipe for Traditional Macaroni & Cheese courtesy of Nestlé. Used with permission.

PAGE 88 National Pork Board: Recipe for Broiled Grits Wedges courtesy of the National Pork Board. Used with permission.

PAGE 89 Wisconsin Milk Marketing Board: Recipe for Seafood Risotto courtesy of © 2004 Wisconsin Milk Marketing Board, Inc. Used with permission.

PAGES 90/91 McCormick: Photo and recipe for Herbed Bread Stuffing courtesy of McCormick. Used with permission.

PAGE 92 Sargento: Photo and recipe for Mexican Mini Quiches courtesy of Sargento Foods Inc. Used with permission.

PAGE 93 McCormick: Recipe for Corn Pudding courtesy of McCormick. Used with permission.

PAGE 93 Tone Brothers: Recipe for Grilled Portobello Mushrooms courtesy of Tone Brothers, Inc., producer of Tone's, Spice Islands, and Durkee products. Used with permission.

PAGE 94 Bruce Foods: Recipe for Holiday Yams & Pecans courtesy of Bruce Foods Corporation. Used with permission.

PAGE 95 Sargento: Photo and recipe for Cheesy Stuffed Mushrooms courtesy of Sargento Foods Inc. Used with permission.

PAGE 96 Florida Tomato Committee: Photo and recipe for Tomato and Potato Casserole courtesy of Florida Tomato Committee. Used with permission.

PAGE 97 Kraft Foods: Recipe for Pot of Black-eyed Peas courtesy of Kraft Kitchens. Used with permission.

PAGE 97 Sargento: Recipe for Cheese Dipped Veggie courtesy of Sargento Foods Inc. Used with permission.

PAGES 98/99 Sargento: Photo and recipe for Cheddar-Stuffed Spuds courtesy of Sargento Foods Inc. Used with permission.

PAGE 100 French's: Recipe for Spinach Pie courtesy of French's® French Fried Onions. Used with permission.

PAGE 101 Kraft Foods: Recipe for Stuffed Acorn Squash Rings courtesy of Kraft Kitchens. Used with permission.

WEB SITES

PAGES 102/103 Florida Tomato Committee: Photo and recipe for Tomato Stuffed with Couscous courtesy of the Florida Tomato Committee. Used with permission.

PAGE 104 Kraft Foods: Photo for Parmesan Garlic Bread courtesy of Kraft Kitchens. Used with permission.

PAGE 106 Bruce Foods: Recipe for Sweet Potato Biscuits courtesy of Bruce Foods Corporation. Used with permission.

PAGE 107 Sargento: Photo and recipe for Cheddar Onion Biscuits courtesy of Sargento Foods Inc. Used with permission.

PAGES 108/109 Land O'Lakes: Photo and recipe for Parmesan Bacon Biscuit Sticks courtesy of Land O'Lakes, Inc. Used with permission.

PAGE 110 Land O'Lakes: Photo and recipe for Tender Popovers courtesy of Land O'Lakes, Inc. Used with permission.

PAGE 111 Kraft Foods: Recipe for Parmesan Garlic Bread courtesy of Kraft Kitchens. Used with permission.

PAGES 112/113 Nestlé: Photo and recipe for Bread Machine Garlic Dinner Rolls courtesy of Nestlé. Used with permission.

PAGE 114 Wisconsin Milk Marketing Board: Recipe for Cheese Twists courtesy of the © 2004 Wisconsin Milk Marketing Board, Inc. Used with permission.

PAGE 115 Sargento: Recipe for Zesty Spinach Bread courtesy of Sargento Foods Inc. Used with permission.

PAGE 116 B&G Foods: Recipe for Fiesta Cornbread courtesy of B&G Foods. Used with permission.

PAGE 117 Almond Board of California: Recipe for Roasted Garlic Toast courtesy of the Almond Board of California. Used with permission.

PAGES 118/119 Dole: Photo and recipe for Classic Banana Bread courtesy of Dole Food Company. Used with permission.

PAGE 120 Ocean Spray Cranberries: Recipe for Cranberry Almond Bread courtesy of Ocean Spray Cranberries, Inc. Used with permission.

PAGE 121 Tone Brothers: Recipe for Asiago Bread courtesy of Tone Brothers, Inc., producer of Tone's, Spice Islands, and Durkee products. Used with permission.

PAGES 122/123 Kraft Foods: Photo and recipe for Irish Soda Bread courtesy of Kraft Kitchens. Used with permission.

PAGE 124 Nestlé: Photo for Sweet Potato Pies courtesy of Nestlé. Used with permission.

PAGE 126 Sunkist: Recipe for Caramelized Orange Flan courtesy of Sunkist Growers, Inc. Used with permission.

PAGE 127 Wisconsin Milk Marketing Board: Recipe for Wisconsin Brie & Fruit Pie courtesy of the © 2004 Wisconsin Milk Marketing Board, Inc. Used with permission.

PAGE 127 Almond Board of California: Recipe for Raisin & Almond Risotto courtesy of the Almond Board of California. Used with permission.

PAGE 128 National Honey Board: Recipe for Golden Pear Gratin courtesy of the National Honey Board. Used with permission.

PAGE 129 National Honey Board: Recipe for Honey Baked Apples courtesy of the National Honey Board. Used with permission.

PAGE 130 National Honey Board: Recipe for Fruit Salad with Honey-Orange Dressing courtesy of the National Honey Board. Used with permission.

PAGE 130 McCormick: Recipe for Winter Fruit Compote courtesy of McCormick. Used with permission.

PAGE 131 French's: Recipe for Scalloped Apples & Onions courtesy of French's® French Fried Onions. Used with permission.

PAGES 132/133 Kraft Foods: Photo and recipe for White Chocolate Bread Pudding courtesy of Kraft Kitchens. Used with permission.

PAGE 134 Land O'Lakes: Photo and recipe for Old-Fashioned Bread Pudding with Vanilla Sauce courtesy of Land O'Lakes, Inc. Used with permission.

PAGE 135 USA Rice Federation: Recipe for Cinnamon Rice Pudding courtesy of USA Rice Federation. Used with permission.

PAGE 136 Kraft Foods: Photo and recipe for 15-Minute Autumn Rice Pudding courtesy of Kraft Kitchens. Used with permission.

PAGE 137 Almond Board of California: Recipe for Almond Tuille Cookie Cups courtesy of the Almond Board of California. Used with permission.

PAGES 138/139 Nestlé: Photo and recipe for Sweet Potato Pies courtesy of Nestlé. Used with permission.

RODALE INC.
www.rodale.com

Almond Board of California
www.almondsarein.com

American Egg Board
www.aeb.org

B&G Foods
www.bgfoods.com

Bird's Eye Foods
www.birdseyefoods.com

Bruce Foods
www.brucefoods.com

California Strawberry Commission
www.calstrawberry.com

CanolaInfo
www.canolainfo.org

Cherry Marketing Institute
www.usacherries.com

Dole Food Company
www.dole.com

Earthbound Farms
www.earthboundfarm.com

Florida Tomato Commission
www.floridatomatoes.org

French's
www.frenchsfoods.com

Kraft Foods
www.kraftfoods.com

Land O'Lakes, Inc.
www.landolakes.com

McCormick
www.mccormick.com

Michigan Asparagus Advisory Board
www.asparagus.com

National Honey Board
www.honey.com

National Pork Board
www.otherwhitemeat.com

Nestlé
www.meals.com,
www.verybestbaking.com

Ocean Spray Cranberries
www.oceanspray.com

Produce for Better Health Foundation
www.5aday.org

Sargento
www.sargentocheese.com

Sunkist
www.sunkist.com

Tone Brothers
www.spiceadvice.com

Uncle Ben's
www.unclebens.com

United States Potato Board
www.potatohelp.com

USA Rice Federation
www.usarice.com

Wisconsin Milk Marketing Board
www.wisdairy.com

Wish-Bone
www.wish-bone.com

INDEX

✔ Designates a SuperQuick recipe that gets you in and out of the kitchen in 30 minutes or less!
Boldface page numbers refer to photographs. *Italicized* page numbers refer to boxed text.